THE
LEGAL BEAGLE
LAW BOOK

Bill Thomas is a solicitor who lives and practises in North Norfolk. He is a journalist, author and broadcaster.

He is the author of 'Questions of Law'; editor of the 'Encyclopaedia of Consumer Law'; and co-author with his wife Ann Foster of 'The Retail Handbook'.

He acts for and advises retailers and manufacturers, and is a member of the Legal Advisory Panel of the National Consumer Council. He has devoted the last 14 years to what has become known as 'consumer law' and to trying to make it mean something to the men and women most affected by it — the general public.

Most weeks he is heard on BBC Radio 2's Jimmy Young Programme and appears regularly on BBC 2 in 'East on Two'.

He is married with two sons, a dog and three cats.

THE
LEGAL BEAGLE
LAW BOOK

Bill Thomas
'The Legal Beagle'
of
Radio 2's Jimmy Young Programme
and BBC's East on Two

ISBN   0–7117–0273–X

© Copyright W H Thomas 1986.

Illustrations by Tony Hall

Designed and produced by Parke Sutton Limited,
Norwich
for
Jarrold Colour Publications, Norwich
Printed in England

Contents

Introduction

I am often asked — why the 'Legal Beagle'? The answer goes back a long way to the days when I first started on BBC Radio 2. Lawyers who then appeared on the Jimmy Young Programme were called 'Legal Eagles'. In August 1975 I acquired my beagle – Robinson. A bit later I mentioned this on the air and said that I supposed that made me (or him) a "Legal Beagle". The name stuck — even eleven years later that is how I am known to many listeners — especially lawyers!

I have found that some legal questions are asked time and time again. This book is intended to guide readers through the legal maze surrounding these most common areas of legal uncertainty and to give answers which make the law intelligible.

Obviously the advice that I can give is general. Detailed answers require detailed information which space does not permit. If you are in any doubt please consult a solicitor or at least see the Citizens' Advice Bureau which provides so much help. Also I have avoided anything to do with crime or housing or tax.

The laws in Scotland and Northern Ireland may be different. So this book is limited in its legal application to England and Wales — though people living in other parts of the United Kingdom may still find some general guidance.

Bill Thomas

Shopping

1 **The Sale of Goods Act is supposed to give shoppers legal rights. What are these rights — and why is it that many retailers simply refer you to the manufacturer and appear to wash their hands when there is a problem with faulty goods?**

The law in Sections 13 and 14 of the Sale of Goods Act 1979 is nice and clear. When goods are sold in the course of a business they **must** correspond with any description, be of 'merchantable quality' and be 'fit for their intended use'. These obligations are imposed on all retailers of goods and cannot be avoided. It is **their** responsibility to ensure that what they sell meets the law. And if there is a problem — it is the **trader's** legal duty to deal with your complaint. If the defect is sufficient to make the stuff useless — your remedy is your money back there and then.

The retailer has exactly the same legal rights as you have; so he can make an identical claim against the manufacturer or other person who supplied him. There may be some restriction on his ability to pursue his legal claim. But that does not in any way reduce the retailer's legal obligations. It's not his 'fault' that what he has sold is duff; but it is his responsibility to deal with the problem.

You have no legal claim against the manufacturer because the contract of sale was between you and the retailer. So if the shop tries to fob you off by telling you to take it up with the manufacturer — don't be taken for a ride.

2 **Why do some shops insist on the production of a receipt before dealing with complaints?**

There is some sympathy with those retailers who say that if they are not careful, they get ripped off by dodgy customers. Apparently some crooked people buy (or steal or 'come by') something. Then they take it to a shop selling it at a high price and ask for their money back. Therefore, to avoid this sort of fraud, the shop asks for a receipt to be produced. So far so good. The trouble is that most of us are **not** crooks. And the tiny little bits of paper that many shops now hand out and call receipts (and expect us to hang on to for several weeks or months) are quite unsuitable. If a shop wants a document to be retained it should ensure that it is large, easily identified as a receipt and bear some legend such as **'KEEP THIS SAFE'**. Again the law is clear. If you say you have a complaint you have to 'prove' that it was the shop that sold you the goods. You prove this by production of a receipt, or a cheque stub, or a credit card voucher or a guarantee card — but if you have not got any of this — your **word** is extremely good evidence. If you have not retained your receipt and have no other 'proof' — insist on your word being taken seriously.

3 **Do I need a receipt if what I want is a replacement because I have changed my mind?**

All the legal rights mentioned refer to goods which are **faulty**. In that case the retailer is **always** liable to you. But his legal duty extends no further than that. If you buy something and when you get home you don't like it (or your spouse turns away in pain when shown it) and you want to return it — you have to think carefully. The shop is under no legal obligation to take back your mistakes — unless, of course, they said they would when you bought the goods. So if you ask for a refund or a replacement the shop is doing you a favour — and can insist on a receipt; make a 'handling charge'; or offer you a credit note. It's up to you to decide what you want. Of course some shops make it a matter of policy always to refund money if goods are returned in pristine condition — although many now insist on a receipt if the price was more than a stated figure.

4 **A friend gave me a food-processor for a present. After a couple of months it broke. I took it back to the shop but they said that as I had no 'proof of purchase' they were not bound to do anything. They refuse to honour the guarantee and I think it is unfair. What can I do?**

Well the shop is strictly correct, at least in saying that it has no legal obligation to **you.** The gadget was bought by your friend — and so the contract (which contains all the Sale of Goods Act remedies) was between him and the shop. You have no legal relationship with the shop, hence no legal remedies. It would have been different if your pal had added to the label —

*To Agnes with my fondest love — **and my rights under the Sale of Goods Act 1979***

This would have transferred his right to you and enabled you to make a claim. He would have had to give the shop notice of the gift and the transfer of the

rights. A bit daft, you may think — but that's the law
for you. Of course the guarantee may help you, but that
is not a legal thing at all.

5
I bought a hair-dryer with a 'money-off'
coupon from a magazine. It didn't work
properly but the shop will not give me
anything else in return as they say that I only
paid part of the price myself. Surely the
normal rules still apply?

Absolutely. This is a perfectly straight-forward sale of
goods, the 'consideration' for which was partly good
old money and partly a bit of paper. If the goods were
defective, you have all the usual rights under the Sale
of Goods Act 1979 to be able to claim your money back
(if the defect was serious and occurred shortly after
purchase) or to the cost of a repair. You should explain
to the owner of the shop that simply because he accepts
coupons or vouchers in part payment does not reduce
his absolute liability for the quality and fitness of what
he sells. You would be entitled to the *full* price of the
hair-dryer, since a mere refund of your money would
not enable you to buy another similar one. Even if the
coupon had 'paid' for the whole price you would still
have been protected. Under the Supply of Goods and
Service Act 1982 there are identical rules to those for
the sale of goods to enable customers to get redress.

6
Just what is the status of a guarantee?

It's a bit of paper with writing on it. The majority of
guarantees are given by the manufacturers of goods.
They may confer certain benefits but almost certainly
they have no legal standing at all. Because you buy
goods from a shop it is with that **shop** that you have the
contract. But you have no contract with the
manufacturer since he did not sell to you nor give you
anything in return for money. So what legal remedies

you have are always against the person who sold the article. (You may, under very restricted circumstances, have a claim against the manufacturer if you can show he was to **blame** for a defect — but that is almost impossible to prove.) If a fault develops, whether you go back to the shop, or rely on the guarantee, really depends on what the fault is and how it was caused. And try to read the terms of the guarantee **before** you buy the goods. That's often difficult because the card is at the bottom of a sealed box. As some are so limited in what they offer, you may wish to buy something with a better guarantee.

7 **I recently bought a kettle from a large electrical store. After a few days it stopped working. When I took it back, the shop insisted on sending it off for inspection and repairs saying it would take some days. After a week I rang to be told that it wasn't ready and I should use a saucepan. Two weeks later I am still 'kettleless'. What can I do?**

So long as the fault was due to a defect in the kettle — and not because you dropped it or tried to cook fish in it — the shop is clearly responsible. It **must** refund your money — plus your out of pocket expenses in getting the kettle back to the shop. Send a seven-day letter:-
If you do not meet your obligations under the Sale of Goods Act 1979 within seven days from today — I shall issue a summons in the local county court. And send them a copy of this book!

8 **When I returned some faulty goods to a shop, the owner refused to give me a refund but offered a 'credit note' to spend in his shop within a month. I did not want this; indeed I never want to buy from him again. Am I stuck with this credit note?**

No; certainly not. The trader is in the same legal position as in the last question. So long as the goods are defective and have not been misused — he **must** refund the money. Same advice — a seven-day letter.

9 Having bought a jumper in a sale I discovered it was torn and fraying at a seam. The shop says that it was in a sale — what did I expect. Are sale goods outside the usual laws?

Certainly not. The fact that something is in a 'sale' is merely an indication that it is cheaper than it was — **not** that it is sub-standard or lacking some essential feature. So the usual law in the Sale of Goods Act 1979 applies to sale goods in exactly the same way as for new things. If the shop **knows** that there is something wrong with goods — there is nothing to stop it indicating this by a label saying 'torn'; 'shop-soiled'; 'only one arm' — anything that is **true**. Then you will have been told why the price was reduced and would have no legal claim.

10 I recently bought a dress in a sale — but I have now discovered that the price I was charged was not reduced at all from the normal price. Have I any come-back?

First — the word 'SALE' suggests to a law-enforcement officer that prices **will** be reduced from what they were before. So unless the shop clearly indicated that this particular dress was **not** in the sale, they have committed a criminal offence under the Trade Descriptions Act 1968. This says that it is a crime to indicate that a price is reduced from a 'normal' price when it is not. So you can report the shop to the Trading Standards Department who may take action against it. But you may not get your excess price back since under the **civil** law no wrong has been done. They showed a price; you paid it. If the shop is prosecuted, you can ask the court to order the shop to refund the difference to you when it passes sentence on the guilty trader.

11 I got a leaflet through the door inviting me to join a book club. They said if I was not satisfied I could get my money back by returning the books within 28 days. I changed my mind and did what they said within the time limit. The club says it did not receive the books in time and refuse to refund my money. Is there anything I can do?

Of course. You can take them to court. Write to the Managing Director of the outfit — by name — and ask him if this is the way he carries on business all the time. If he says 'yes' you should issue a county court summons against the company claiming your money back. Once the books were put in the post to be sent back to the club, the legal ownership of the books passed back to the club. So it's **their** problem if they were lost or delayed in the post.

12 I ordered some goods by mail order, and sent off part payment. Then the company asked me to pay the balance — which I did. I didn't receive the goods or hear anything from the company. After some time, I made enquiries and discovered the company had gone bust. How do I get my money back?

By waiting and keeping your fingers crossed. Probably you will get nothing at all and if you look on it as money down the drain — anything that does come your way will be a bonus. Many mail order companies rely on pre-payments to buy in the stock which they offer in their catalogues. So if they have ordered goods from a supplier which goes out of business — there goes your money. It is important that you try and find out from the Official Receiver (a government chap who deals initially with failed companies) who has been appointed 'liquidator'. Then write to the liquidator, keeping a copy of your letter, setting out the details of the money you paid and asking for a 'proof of debt' form so that you can register your claim. **But** — if the company has **no** assets there is **no** money to repay its debts.

Moral: Never pay in advance for anything.

13 Recently I have had a spate of things delivered to me that I have not ordered. Either someone is filling in coupons using my name, or traders are selecting me for possible sales and sending things in the hope that I pay. What can I do to stop it?

The simplest thing is to use the remedies in the Unsolicited Goods and Services Act 1971. This allows you to do one of two things. Either write to the trader, giving your name and address and identifying the goods and saying that they were sent to you without your asking for them. The trader then has *one month* in which to collect the goods (or he can send you a pre-paid label so that you can send them back to him).

Or, you do nothing at all for *six months*. After that time
the goods become yours to do with as you wish.
Obviously you do have to keep them for the whole of
the six months and be prepared to allow the trader to
have them if he asks for them during that period. If he
is foolish enough to threaten to sue for the unpaid price
— the answer is quite simple. You do not pay as the
goods were unsolicited.

14 After buying a three-piece suite and getting it
home I changed my mind because it did not fit
the scheme in my living room. I stopped the
cheque. Now a friend says I am in the wrong
and the shop is entitled to the money. How can
this be? They have not lost anything.

Oh yes they have. They have lost the value of the sale to
you. You are in breach of contract — because one of
the **shopper's** legal obligations under the Sale of Goods
Act 1979 is to take delivery and pay for goods bought.
The shop can therefore sue you for the price. And by
'stopping' the cheque you have helped them because
legally you have 'dishonoured a bill of exchange'. This
gives them the right to 'sue on the cheque'. If you can
persuade the shop to take the goods back — remember
they have **no** legal obligation to do so — expect to pay
them the loss of profit on the transaction.
   Moral: **never** stop a cheque simply because you have
changed your mind. It is only permissible **if** and **only** if
there is a clear breach of contract by the supplier.

15 I tried to buy some furniture on hire-purchase
but the shop said my credit-rating wasn't good,
although I have never been in debt. Where do
they get this sort of information and is there
any way I can see what is said about me and
clear my name?

Yes. They get the dope from 'credit reference agencies'
— companies which receive and store information
about most of us and the way we deal with money and
debt. The shop says that Mrs. Snooks wants credit for,

say £750; the credit-reference agency looks through its
register to see if she is there and gives them a report.
There is nothing wrong with this sort of checking.
Would **you** lend money to a complete stranger without
finding out about him?

Under the Consumer Credit Act 1974 you have a
right to find out what the agency knows about you.
There is a sequence to be followed. You have to ask the
shop **in writing** to tell you the name and address of the
credit reference agency. They **must** give you this within
seven working days. You can then write to the agency
with a fee of £1 asking for a copy of the 'file' which they
have on you — and they must give you a copy within
seven working days. (It's a criminal offence for the
shop or the agency to refuse to deal with your
requests.) If there is anything on the file which you
don't agree with, or is wrong, (they may have got you
muddled with some other person) you have the right to
ask for a correction or deletion. And if the agency
won't accept what you say, you can appeal to the Office
of Fair Trading to sort it out.

16 I bought a used car privately after reading a small ad in the local paper. Both the advert and the guy selling the car said it was 'in perfect working order' but I have found several faults. I still have the advert — do I have any claim against the seller for false pretences?

Not for 'false pretences' which suggests some sort of
criminal intent. But you **do** have a civil law claim
under Section 13 of the Sale of Goods Act 1979. The
words 'in perfect working order' can be said to amount
to a description of the car — and having found the
faults you have proof that it was **not** in perfect
condition. The faults must be serious, of course, and of
a sort which the seller would have known about; not
things which happened after you bought it and drove
thousands of miles! You can sue the seller for your
money back — but before you do, make certain that he

still lives at the address you have, and that he has a job
and assets. There is no point in taking a man of straw to
court.

17 **Talking about 'private' sales, there is a man
who lives near me who is always advertising
private cars for sale claiming that they are his
own and that he is not a trader. Would a buyer
of one of these cars have any legal claim if
there was a problem with the car?**

Because of people like this who mask business
activities by pretending to be private sellers, the law
was changed in 1977. Adverts must now indicate
whether the sale is 'in the course of a business' or not.
If the advert says nothing, it is assumed that it is a
private sale. But if it then appears that the 'private'
seller inserts dozens of adverts for many cars without
indicating that he is in business, you can report the
facts to the Trading Standards Department, which may
take the man to court. More to the point, showing that
he is in reality a trader enables you to sue him for
breach of the Sale of Goods Act 1979 — because the car
is not of 'merchantable quality' or 'fit for its intended
use'.

18 **A number of local shops have signs saying 'no
money back' or 'no goods exchanged'. Why do
they do this and are they, in fact, allowed to do
it?**

It is illegal, a criminal offence carrying a fine of up to
£2000. Shops do it because they do not want to meet
their unavoidable obligations under the Sale of Goods
Act 1979 — although they try to disguise this fact by
saying that of course they will deal with complaints,
but do not want to allow people to change their minds.
The short answer to that is that the notice should spell
out exactly what they really mean. 'We will gladly
deal with complaints about defects in what you buy
from us but will not make refunds or exchanges to
customers who change their minds and wish to

return their mistakes' would be a more honest way of trading.

19 What happens to shoes left at a repairer and never collected?

If the shoe-repairer has his wits about him (and they usually do) he will ensure that it is a term of the contract between him and the customer that if no collection takes place within, say, 14 days, he can dispose of the shoes. Then he can do just that — although he can only retain the cost of the repair and has to account to the owner for the balance. Other than that, he will have to use the procedure laid down in the Torts (Interference with Goods) Act, 1977 which requires notices to be served on the owner of the uncollected stuff. This means that the name and address has to be noted and kept. Otherwise the trader has to apply to the court for permission to sell the goods. Again, he has to account to the owner for any change after the costs of the repair and sale by auction have been met.

20 In a local store car-park there is a sign which says 'Cars parked at owner's risk — no liability for death or injury or any other loss or damage'. I thought this sort of sign had been outlawed.

There is nothing illegal about putting up this sort of sign, but the law has now limited their effectiveness. No business can avoid its liability for death or injury caused by **its** negligence. So the sign would be useless to protect the store if someone was hurt because of some act or mistake by the store or its staff. Apart from that, the store is saying that it has no responsibility if your car is damaged in some other way — eg by some other fool driving into it. But the store would not be liable for that anyway. So one wonders why they bother with the cost of putting up the sign. It is probably there to try and dissuade you from making a claim in the event of the store **actually** being the cause of injury or damage. In such a case **don't** be put off bringing a claim.

21 Talking of signs, I recently broke a glass ornament in a china shop. There was a sign saying 'All breakages must be paid for'. Do I have to pay up? You can't see these things unless you pick them up to have a close look.

Normally one expects to be able to touch goods in shops. But if the trader wants to prevent this — and, after all, it's his property — he can put up this sort of notice. By doing so he is telling you not to 'trespass on his goods' — literally — and if you do so and damage them, then he can ask for the money as 'damages for trespass'. The same goes for 'do not squeeze me until I am yours' signs on greengrocery shelves. It's a fair warning to you. Also one way of discouraging trade!

22 I bought a soft toy for my two-year old. She played with it for a couple of hours, then one of the eyes came off. It was fixed by a sharp pin. Fortunately I saw it in time and was able

to take it away — but she could have
swallowed the eye with awful consequences or
injured herself with the pin. There was
nothing on the label to say it wasn't suitable
for two-year olds. Surely this sort of
hazardous toy should be banned?

You can report the facts to the Trading Standards
Department who can take action against the shop (and
everyone else in the chain of distribution) for selling
(or even stocking) things like this which are potentially
dangerous to children. Safety Regulations are in force
dealing with many aspects of the safety of toys,
especially for very young children. If bits can be pulled
off or sharp or cutting insides can be exposed on any
'child's plaything' — there is a breach of these
Regulations. The same rules also limit, very severely,
the contents of paint used to decorate toys — restricting
the poisonous elements — the voltages of battery
operated toys, and cover the flammability of furry toys.
But, curiously, they have been held not to cover things
like the novelty dolls you might bring home as a
souvenir — on the basis that they are not 'children's
playthings'.

23 I bought a washing machine on hire-purchase.
My husband has just been made redundant
and I don't see how we can keep up the
payments. Will the shop let us miss a few
months' instalments, or pay less?

First — are you sure that it **is** hire-purchase? The legal
situation may differ if you are actually involved in
another form of credit. In HP, you go to a shop and
select a machine. The shops **sells** it to a finance house
which in turn 'hires' it to you. So your legal
relationship is with the finance house **not** the shop.
Any action you want to take must be with the finance
house direct. Don't go to the shop and ask for help; deal
with the lender.
    Next — do not **under any circumstances** simply stop
paying. You will be regarded as a defaulter and the

machinery for dealing with people who don't pay will
be put into action. It may take a lot of effort and
expense to stop that particular wagon from rolling. No
legal action can be started against you without your
being sent a notice. If you have paid at least one-third
of the total price, no one can take possession of the
goods without a court order. If you decide that it might
be better to end the HP agreement, you are entitled to
do so by giving notice to the finance house and by
paying enough to make half the total price (taking into
account all you have paid already). You have to return
the goods, of course. Finally, it is always open to you
and the lender to agree a variation of the original
agreement. This may be done by substituting a new HP
for smaller payments but for a longer time. The vital
thing is to write and explain your new circumstances
and ask for help — and do keep a copy of your letters.

24 I was given some gift-vouchers for use at a
health club. I couldn't use them for a while as
the club was fully booked. When I finally got
an appointment and turned up, the club said
the vouchers were out of date — they could
only be used for three months. As it was past
that limit, I could not use them. There was
nothing printed on the vouchers about date or
time limits. But the club still would not let me
use them. Are they right?

This sounds a bit of a con — but they are probably
right. They issued the gift-vouchers and can specify the
terms and conditions in which they can be used. But
one would have thought that if time was so important
to them — and to potential users — they would have
spelled it out on the vouchers. As nothing was said,
you could argue that it should be possible to use the
vouchers for an indefinite time; that would be met with
the counter-argument that they had to be used within a
'reasonable time' — and that three months *is*
reasonable. There is little that you can do legally; the
best thing is to vote with your feet and take your

custom elsewhere. If enough people did that, the club would get the message. Many health clubs are 'here today and gone tomorrow' and they use gimmicks like 'free' vouchers to attract would-be members, who then pay a large fee but find that the club packs up before the end of the year. Stick to gardening!

25 What is the difference between a quotation and an estimate?

A 'quotation' is **the price** at which the trader will do the job; no more, no less. If he wants to charge VAT on top, he must say so at the time he gives the quotation; otherwise one can assume that the quote is a tax-inclusive price. An 'estimate' is what the word sounds like — a pretty good indication of what the price will be — but giving leeway up or down (funny how it's usually up, isn't it!). So the final bill may vary by, say, ten per cent. And **never** pay anything in advance — unless, perhaps, you get something tangible and which belongs to you — like bricks or building materials or rolls of electrical cable, for example. Then if the contractor defaults at least you have something which you can try and sell to recover some of your misspent money.

26 My neighbour bought a tarpaulin at an auction. It was described as being 45 feet by 25 feet — but when he got it home and unrolled it for the first time he found it was half that size. What can he do?

There was a misrepresentation by the auctioneer which means that the buyer can return the goods and recover his money. Only if your attention is drawn to a potential problem — as when goods are catalogued as being 'as found' or 'believed to be of the school of J S Cotman' are you warned that the stuff is probably broken, riddled with woodworm or really painted by someone's aunt on a wet afternoon.

27 Although a local trader has a credit-card 'logo' in the doorway he refused to accept mine when I offered to pay for goods with it. He said he would only take cash from me. Is this right?

The basic law is that a trader can insist on cash; nothing else. But in this day and age paying by cheque is perfectly acceptable — so long as one can offer a cheque guarantee card to back any sum up to £50. On the other hand, if the trader implies by showing the sign or logo that he will take credit cards, he must do so or risk breaking the Trade Descriptions Act 1968. Also, the credit card company will not be at all happy. The only justifiable reason for refusing would be if he checked with the card firm and was told that your card had been withdrawn or you had exceeded the credit limit. But, if this is the case, he should tell you so.

28 I took my car to the garage for a service and to have minor faults repaired. They said it would be 'about £60 plus parts and VAT'. The final bill was £180 plus parts and tax. They said this was because the work was trickier than they had expected. When I said I wouldn't pay, they refused to let me take *my* car away. Is this something I just have to take lying down?

Last point first; anyone who is owed money and who has temporary possession of the debtor's goods has what lawyers call a 'lien'. This is the legal right to retain custody until payment. That's why the garage would not let you drive home; the car was security for the money owed by you. On the main point, where a garage gives an estimate for work, it is supposed to have some idea of what needs to be done and so give you a figure which reflects its skill and expertise and is reasonably close to the final bill. It may be out by ten per cent or so — but not by this vast discrepancy. Either refuse to pay — in which case you may have difficulty in getting the car back; or pay up on sufferance explaining firmly and politely that on your way home you will be calling in at the county court to issue a summons for the recovery of the money. Court fees are paid by the loser — and may well be an incentive to a difficult trader to pay up quietly.

29 I am having an extension built and obtained an estimate from a glazier. This was very competitive and I accepted it. While the glass was actually being fitted, the glazier said he had underestimated the size of the glass because the door was different from the one from which he took the measurements. I told him that it was his problem, not mine — but he said he would not fit another inch of glass unless I agreed to pay. Should I?

On the face of it this is straight-foward; if he has made a blunder over measuring the door — then he has to stand the loss. But was he actually shown the right door by you or your builder? Did you say you 'thought' it **might** be type A or B or whatever, on the layman's ignorant basis that one door is much like another? If there is any doubt about what happened when the estimate was being prepared, and if the original bid was a good one, and the new price is still competitive — accept the situation and pay up.

Moral: It's better to lose £10 than to have no door.

30 One evening we were visited by a double-glazing salesman. A nice young man — but he stayed and stayed, even though we made it clear that we did not want the stuff. Finally, after midnight, just to get rid of him, we signed some bit of paper he gave us and let him have a cheque for £100 as a preliminary deposit. This was also said to be 'subject to survey'. We felt safe because the salesman said that if we changed our minds we could cancel. The next morning I wrote to the company to do just that — but they have written back to say they won't accept my cancellation and that the salesman had no authority to say that we could. They

refuse to refund our money and say a man will be coming soon to measure up. We had wondered about paying by instalments. Have we any rights?

There are a number of dodgy salesmen about who will make all sorts of promises to get a sale. To try and prevent this, the company's forms will have lots of small print, among which will be some wording to the effect that 'these terms cannot be altered except in writing and signed by a director'. This is to nullify any promises made to you by the salesman. Probably, the salesman's words would be a 'representation' which induced you to make the contract. If it can be shown that the 'representation' was wrong — then you can get out of the contract. So the answer is to write to the company again, keeping a copy, saying that you relied on their salesman's promise and that as this turns out to be wrong, you are repudiating the contract and will they please send you the £100. If they don't, then it's off to the county court.

Beware of the words 'subject to survey'. It has been held in two cases — one about a house and the other actually about double-glazing — the words do **not** enable one to get out of the contract on the basis that a survey has not yet been done. So don't allow yourself to be gulled into thinking that you are safe if the man says "We'll just put 'subject to survey' so that you are protected". You are not.

If only you *had* ticked the box about credit. Once you say that you want to pay by credit terms you are hugely protected. When the agreement is made away from trade premises — like in your home — there are a series of procedural steps which **have** to be gone through and the company has to send you copies of the completed agreement. Then you still have five days *after* you receive the second copy of the agreement through the post in which to cancel — and get back any money paid.

Moral: **Never** sign anything to get rid of a salesman. **Never** sign a document you have not read and understood — tell the man you want legal advice. If he is reputable he will understand. **Always** tick the 'credit' box if someone is selling in your house — it automatically gives you a 'cooling-off' period.

31

I rented a television from Company *A*. I was disappointed with their service, so I changed to Company *B* — who were very good. After a couple of years I was amazed to get a letter from Company *B* saying that they had 'teamed up' with their sister company *A* which would be dealing with all TV rental. Can companies just deal with my hire agreement like this and can I cancel immediately?

Yes they can and no you can't — not immediately anyway. Anyone who has some usable benefit can 'assign' it to someone else. The commonest example is when a company will 'sell' its bad debts to a collection firm. To make this legal, the first company must give notice to the customer — and this they did. Your TV agreement is **probably** on a yearly basis which means you can only end it when the year runs out. But it might be terminable on a month's notice — in which case you can give this amount of notice and bring the thing to an end. Read the hiring agreement and its small print. It should spell it out for you.

32

I am having difficulty in taking action against a local trader because I don't know his name. He sells pet food and the shop is called 'Dog's Dinner'. The man answers to the name of 'Reg' but no other details are available. How can I find out?

The Business Names Act 1985 requires **every** trader — whether he is on his own, in a partnership, or trades as a limited company — who uses any name which is not his *own*, or the full name of the company, to do two things.

First: he **must** display at his premises a prominent notice, easily read by customers stating — (a) his full

name or the full name of each partner or the full name
of limited company; and (b) an address in the United
Kingdom where documents may be served.

The sort of notice will look like this.

Business Names Act 1985
BILL'S BEAGLE BAR
Owner: William Henry Thomas and
Rupert Patrick Green

Address for service of documents:
246 High Road Diss Norfolk

---

or

Business Names Act 1985
WASHETERIA
Owners: R and J Launderettes Limited
Address for service of documents: The Old Laundry
Wolverhampton West Midlands

Secondly, this information **must** be shown on all
business letters, written orders for goods or services,
invoices and receipts and written demands for the
payment of business debts.

Any trader — Reg included — who fails to do this
commits a criminal offence, for which the fine is up to
£200. It's also worth bearing in mind that if a trader
brings an action against a customer who can prove
that: he was unable to make a legal claim against the
trader because of the lack of information, or: he
suffered some financial loss due to his ignorance of the
trader's identity — the case is likely to be thrown out
unless the court thinks it fair to go ahead. So tell Reg to
put up his 'particulars of ownership' sign or else you
will see him in court!

33 I am told that children cannot make contracts, and they have no legal status anyway. What is the law?

Of course they can; they do it all day long — going on buses and trains, visiting football grounds, buying sweets, comics, books, clothes, records, tapes — the list is endless. The only time the law comes into play (to coin a phrase) is if the child buys goods or services but does **not** pay in full. Should the trader want to recover the money by taking the child to court, he would have to prove that what was sold was 'necessary' for the child's well-being. Prudent traders will not sell expensive goods to young children on credit; although to sell a 17-year old a moped might well be perfectly sensible and 'necessary' and therefore be upheld by a court.

34 What do the letters 'APR' in credit advertisements mean?

In short, they stand for the 'Annual Percentage Rate of Charge' which is a formula designed to tell you what is the effective rate of interest you are paying (rather than the *flat* rate, which is what used to be quoted in the days before the Consumer Credit Act 1974 came into force). It has to be advertised so that you have some basis of comparing the cost of different forms of credit. So far so good; the trouble is that the APR will vary according to the length of the credit agreement and the intervals between instalments. Paying the same amount of loan over three years by quarterly, monthly or weekly instalments means three different APRs — though the actual cash you hand over will in total be the same. So it does not mean that the lowest APR is necessarily the cheapest or best for you. It may simply mean that you are paying smallish instalments for many years. A vast amount of work went into drafting the regulations governing the disclosure of the APR, as well as preparing huge books of tables. A recent survey showed that 84 per cent of women questioned and 68 per cent of men, did not know what it meant, though 82 per cent of 16 to 24-year olds did.

35 Then what is the difference between APR and Flat rates on interest?

The easiest way to describe the (almost) unintelligible is to give an example:

If you borrow £100 at 20 per cent interest and agree to repay it at the end of twelve months you have £100 available to you throughout the whole period of the loan. On the last day you pay back £120. The flat rate is 20 per cent; the APR is 20 per cent too.

But if you borrow at 20 per cent interest and repay £10 on the last day of each twelve months — although you have £100 available to you on the first day, by midway through the year you only have about £50 available to use (because you have already paid about half the original loan). So on a yearly basis, the interest of 20 per cent is chargeable, not on the actual sum borrowed, but on the value of the **average** amount of credit you have through the year — which is about £50. The interest you have agreed to pay is £20 — but that as a percentage of £50 is **40 per cent**. The flat rate is 20 per cent but the APR which would have to be quoted in the advert is 40 per cent. Got it? If not, look at a free booklet from the Office of Fair Trading called 'Credit Charges' which explains the whole thing.

36

My local paper recently carried an advert for a local branch of a national chain of DIY stores. It was advertising a range of branded merchandise at discount prices. Two days later I went to the shop but was told they had 'sold out' of the special offer goods I wanted to buy. Is this legal?

If a shop advertises that certain goods are at a reduced price it is implied that they have those goods available generally. If they want to protect themselves they can say 'valid from 20th to 27th May' or 'limited supplies available' or 'only at larger stores' or 'while stocks last'. Then they can show that they realised that the attractiveness of the offer might lead to a run on the line being advertised. Otherwise, inform the Trading Standards Department.

37

Just after leaving a shop, I was accused of stealing and forced to return to the manager's office. There my bag was searched and I had to turn out my pockets. I insisted I was innocent but was only allowed to leave when the manager and the 'detective' found nothing. They didn't even apologise. What can I do?

Sue the shop. While they have a right to detain anyone if there are reasonable grounds for suspecting that that person has committed an offence, should they turn out to be wrong, the shop may be liable to compensate you for 'false imprisonment'. That means preventing you in any way from going about your business. In a recent case an elderly lady was treated in this way, and the police were called and she was taken to the station for questioning. She was awarded over £1200 for the false imprisonment, and for trespass into her handbag which had been grabbed and searched. See a solicitor and get him to write to the shop demanding damages.

38 I recently booked a holiday with a major tour company through a reputable high street travel agent. I paid a deposit. A couple of months before I was due to go away, I called into the agents to pay the balance of the price — only to be told that there was *no* holiday booked for me. They could only offer a much more expensive holiday which I can't afford. Apart from getting my deposit back what else can I do? Surely I can sue the agent for breach of contract.

It's a funny thing about travel agents; no one seems to know with any certainty just what is their legal status. Are they **your** agents; or those of the tour company? Logic would say the latter, since they earn their living from commission paid to them by tour companies. But it has never been decided in a court.

In this case, start off by asserting that they are the **tour operator's** agents; write to the tour company saying that:-

> *Your agents Bloggs & Co accepted my booking and my money to book one of your holidays but you have failed to honour your side of the deal. I am holding you in breach of contract and look to you for damages. These amount to the deposit plus £x for being disappointed and £y for the higher cost of booking another holiday with a different firm.*

See how that goes.

The tour company will probably be unimpressed by your letter. Then you have a go at the agents on the grounds of 'negligence'. They owed you a duty of care

to process your booking properly — and by failing to
do so they have caused you loss and damage. You then
make the same claim against the agents — sueing them
in the county court if need be. You will see why some
people always book their own holidays.

39 I booked a room at a hotel but was unable to go
because of a change in plans. I rang up and
told them but was surprised to get a bill at the
end of the week when I was due to have stayed
there. They said they could not relet my room.
Surely that is their problem?

Not so. **You** are in breach of contract. You made a
booking: that equals a firm contractual obligation on
your part to go and stay there. Although you let them
know that you could not go, they were not legally
required to 'let you off'. They could either release you
from the contract and claim a small sum to compensate
them for your breach of contract; or, as they have done,
they could hold you to the contract and claim the cost
of the room. They would not be entitled to claim the
cost of meals not eaten — but the room charge and
VAT certainly

40 Recently we fixed up a holiday cottage from a
brochure. When we arrived there, the cottage
was nothing like the description and it was
damp, the cooker didn't work properly and
the place was filthy. We paid the full week's
rent in advance. What can we do now we are
back home?

You are entitled to a reasonable standard of
accommodation, and the facilities should at least
match the brochure. It is possible that there is a breach
of the Trade Descriptions Act 1968. Also you have a
civil claim for disappointment. One point to remember;
the standards that people accept as 'reasonable' may
vary. And what is taken for granted in the country —
no mains drainage, uncertain electricity supply, farm
smells and noises (bird scarers, tractors droning away

from dawn until after dark), housemartins nesting and messing under the eaves — may be regarded as totally unacceptable by a fastidious town dweller. Also, some people may find the filth and squalor amusing and something to bore their friends with during long winter nights. But if you are certain that what you say was really the case and the standard was so low as to be actionable — have a go at the owner of the cottage and think about telling the Trading Standards Department about the dodgy brochure.

41 **When we got to the resort of our long awaited holiday we were told that there had been an 'over-booking' and the rooms we had reserved were not available. We complained but had no choice but to take what there was. Can we make a claim from the holiday company now that we are home?**

Of course. Expect them to try and fob you off by saying that as you 'enjoyed a fortnight at the resort of your choice, what are you complaining about; you had a bed and a room so that's it!' Do not allow yourself to be deterred by this approach. There is a clear breach by the holiday firm of their obligations under the contract which they made with you. Only if the accommodation eventually offered was of the same standard (or better) than that originally booked would you have difficulty in showing a judge that you had been adversely affected by the tour operator's breach of contract.

42 **We booked a holiday at a hotel said to be '100 yards' from the beach. When we got there, it was 100 yards alright — but that included a mainline railway (with no crossing) and part of an inner-city by-pass. We had actually to make a two mile journey to get to the sand. Is there any redress against this clear misrepresentation?**

Yes — tell the Trading Standards Department. If there is a statement about a resort in a brochure which is not true at the time the booklet was printed (so that the company knew full well that it was a lie) then it is a criminal offence under the Trade Descriptions Act 1968. You also have a good claim for compensation against the tour company for a 'misrepresentation' about the resort; that means a statement which they made on which you relied when making your contract. Write to the company and claim damages.

43 After an evening meal in a restaurant I was very ill. I am convinced it was because their food was 'off' — but can I prove it and what steps should I take?

Evidence is so often a problem. Was anyone else in your party ill? Did you keep any of the food or any 'samples' for analysis? Because to secure any certainty of action, you must have scientific proof that there is a link between your tummy upset and what you ate. It could be that your lunch or tea was 'off' and it took until after supper for this to come to light. See the problem? On the other hand, salmonella — the bug that causes so much discomfort — is rife in many kitchens. Whether you can actually nail this eating joint is questionable. But it is worth telling the Environmental Health Department because yours may be the latest in a series of complaints which could show a pattern enabling the Council people to investigate.

44 One night at a restaurant we had what can only be described as a nightmare meal. The waiters were rude. They served different food from what we had ordered, then said it was what we had asked for. The bill was high and a 'service charge' was added that did not appear on the menu. When we queried this, large men appeared from the kitchen. We paid up and left — but is there anything we can do?

Several things. First, the food was not of the 'nature, substance or quality demanded' and so means that they have committed an offence under the Food Act 1984. Tell the Environmental Health Department. Secondly, the invented 'service charge' is illegal. Regulations under the Prices Act say that restaurants must show a menu either at the door or where you eat, and that if there is a service charge this must be shown as prominently in the same places. This outfit did not do this — so tell the Trading Standards Department. What else you do depends on your stamina. You could sue them but this would mean having to take the 'large men' to court. Leave it to the enforcement authorities and if there is a court case, ask the magistrates to award you compensation, which would only be the so called service charge — but better than nothing.

45 Is there anything that can be done to stop someone pestering me to pay a bill for work which has not been completed? I had a plumber in to see to the drains; apart from making a filthy mess he has not discovered the

**source of the problem nor has he improved
things by leaving bits of rag in the drain pipes.
Now he keeps sending me bills and bangs on
the door when he passes my house.**

There are two problems here. The first is the defective
drainage system. You must have this put right. Get a
skilled man in to look at the whole thing and tell you
exactly what needs to be done; get an estimate; then get
the job done. The first plumber sounds to be a
charlatan — do not pay him anything at present. If he
keeps on with his demands, write to him pointing out
that under the Administration of Justice Act 1970 it is
an offence to 'harass' a debtor. If he persists, inform
the police and/or the Trading Standards Department.
The plumber may feel aggrieved because you asked
him to do a job beyond his skills or let him tinker with
the problem, rather than employing an expert
specifically to find out what was wrong and then put it
right. Resist his claims and get legal advice if need be.

46 **My bank has missed the payment of one of my
standing orders. This has caused great
embarrassment coupled with the threat of
legal action against me. When I phoned the
bank I was told that it was just one of those
things that happened. Have I any redress?**

Yes. Take your account elsewhere. That is the most
effective step to take (although you may well find that
any other bank is not that different from your own —
whatever the advertising blurb may say!). You have a
relationship of 'debtor-creditor' with your bank. You
leave money with them; they agree to do what you ask.
So if you have funds in your account to cover standing
orders and direct debits, the bank must follow your
instructions. If they don't they are in breach of their
legal duty to you and you have a legal remedy against
them. For example, the failure to pay your standing
order might have looked to an outsider that you were
broke and so reduced your standing in the eyes of right-

thinking people. You could sue for libel; but this would only be done if you were very seriously prejudiced by the bank's failure. It is an indication of the importance which the law attaches to the bank's duty. What you ought to do now, without delay, is to see the manager and tell him what has happened. He will want to keep your custom and may well be able to satisfy you that the error will not be repeated.

47 Is there any rule about how many pennies you can pay with?

Yes, there is a list laid down by statute and amended from time to time to take account both of new coins and (of course) inflation. The current rules are:

20p coins and 50p coins can be used to make a payment up to £10;

5p and 10p coins up to £5; and 1p and 2p coins up to 20p.

£1 coins are legal tender for any amount.

Family Matters

1   **My wife and I have been married for ten years and have no children. We have decided to go our separate ways — there is no one else involved. What is the easiest and cheapest way to obtain a divorce?**

There is only one ground for divorce nowadays — that the marriage has 'irretrievably broken down'. In order to prove this to the court, you have to show at least one of the following circumstances applies:

- that the other spouse has committed adultery and you find it intolerable to live with him or her;
- that the other spouse has been in 'desertion' for at least two years (that means living apart **without** agreement);
- that the other spouse has behaved in such a way that it is unreasonable to expect you to go on living with him or her (what used to be 'cruelty');
- that you have lived apart for two years and **agree** to a divorce;
- that you have lived apart for at least five years.

Therefore you have to be able to bring yourselves within one of these categories — the most usual, where there is no other person involved, being the two years separation. It is essential that you do actually live quite separate lives for the whole of the two year period (though if you try a reconciliation for a few weeks the two year limit does not have to start again; you simply add on the time you spend together seeing if the marriage might still work).

The majority of divorces are done by post — literally. You apply to a divorce court for the necessary forms and send them back; and assuming there are no complications, a date is fixed when the judge will pronounce a 'decree nisi' in open court. Six weeks after that you may apply for a 'decree absolute'. There is a court fee payable to start things off, but nothing to pay after that.

2   What are 'decree nisi' and 'decree absolute'?

A decree 'nisi' means a decree of divorce *unless*' (Latin: nisi = unless) and the 'unless' means that you are divorced 'unless' someone turns up to challenge what has happened. It is not unknown for one spouse to get a divorce by forging the signature of the other spouse; or by claiming that they have lived apart for years when in reality they have been enjoying conjugal bliss. The 'unless' enables anyone who has legitimate grounds to apply to the court to stop the divorce decree. If no one does object or interfere — the decree is made 'absolute' — which finally ends the marriage, leaving each party free to re-marry.

3   Do I need a solicitor for a divorce?

Let's define our terms. 'Divorce' is the means of untying the knot — obtaining from the court a piece of paper which proves you are no longer married. For that step the modern 'postal divorce' system was developed and you do not **need** a solicitor. That does not mean that he cannot be very helpful to you in filling in the forms and advising. But you cannot get full legal aid for divorce itself (unless your spouse claims that the marriage is still going strong and defends your claim for a divorce). Nevertheless there is some financial help. You can see your solicitor on the 'Green Form' legal advice scheme — and many will let you have half an hour's advice for £5. This is often enough to get the divorce under way.

For all other aspects of marital breakdown — children, maintenance, property — a solicitor can be essential and full legal aid is available for this. You have to bear in mind that legal aid is a means-tested benefit — but the limits are more generous than one might think and it is always worth seeing if you do qualify.

4 How soon after a marriage can you get a divorce?

You cannot apply to the court for a divorce until at least one year after the date of your marriage. There are no 'lets or buts' as there used to be before 1984, when the present law came into force.

5 My wife and I have lived apart for three years but never bothered to get a divorce. Now I have met someone whom I want to marry; can I get a divorce?

You can easily do so if your wife consents, if not (and if she will not take action against you on the grounds of your adultery), you will have to wait until you have been apart for five years — then you can get a divorce yourself, and she cannot object.

6 We have been separated for ten months but although I want to re-marry — and freely admit adultery — my wife will not agree to a divorce. What can I do?

Wait until you have been apart for five years. Then divorce **her**

7 My husband is very violent when he has had a drink — which is quite often these days. He has injured me but so far not the children. I am frightened that one day he will do something to them. I can't move out as I have nowhere to go. What can I do?

You can ask the court to make an order (an 'injunction') which makes him leave and stay out of the house and keep away from you and the children. You will need medical evidence of his past attacks — if available; and it helps if there is someone who can give supportive evidence. But don't worry if you cannot think of anyone to back you up; it's an ideal case to take to a solicitor — and he and the court can act with great speed if there is any emergency.

8 What is 'legal separation'?

There is no such thing. It is a phrase used to describe living apart after a court order has been made. If you simply **live** apart — that is 'separation' and it may well be grounds for a divorce in due course. A divorce is obtained at the county court. However, there is wide power for magistrates to deal with some aspects of family life; they make orders for custody, maintenance, and access if you can show that your spouse has deserted you, been cruel, committed adultery or has failed to maintain you or the children. They can also order that you no longer have to live together; this is called a 'non-cohabitation' order and is what many people mean when they talk about getting a 'legal separation'.

9 My wife and I were divorced two years ago. At first things worked out quite well. She kept the children, then aged seven and nine, and I saw them most weekends. But now I have met and moved in with a girl whom I intend to marry. My ex-wife has just 'turned'. She says it is not right that the children should come to my flat as I am 'living in sin'. She keeps finding reasons for the children not to come and won't let them leave her house if my girl-friend is with me — saying that the children are 'naturally very distressed'. I want the children to get to know my girl-friend since we are to be married but it just doesn't seem possible.

You are entitled to reasonable access to your children and if your ex-wife won't be sensible about it you can go back to the court and ask it to define when and how you can see the children. Probably your former wife is jealous of your new-found happiness and is using the

children as a means of getting at you. If it is your
intention to set up home and marry this girl, it is quite
reasonable that you should want to introduce your
children to your new home and, of course, to the lady.
No court would prevent this unless it could be shown
that the girl-friend was quite unsuitable to have contact
with children generally; as this seems most unlikely, go
back to your solicitor and ask him to set in motion an
application to the court. If your ex-wife sees that you
are serious and would actually go to court, she may see
sense.

10 My wife was granted custody of our children.
Although I was given access she refuses point
blank to let them see me. What can I do?

The only thing you can do is to apply to the court to
define access. Courts hate doing this — because once
they lay down a rigid time-table it gives the person
whose unreasonable attitude started the thing off in the
first place further ammunition. Complaints are made if
you are five minutes late or if you have to change the
dates because of illness. And what the children are up
to is also 'used'; one has a party on access day; another
has cubs; or a cold; or sports day; or is revising for
exams… The list of 'genuine' excuses is endless. But if
you are facing a blank wall then going to court is the
only way out. And once your spouse is confronted by a
judge who will see through her, it may be that a proper
long term scheme will be devised.

11 Since our divorce three years ago, my wife has
had custody of our two children. I don't think
she is a very good mother. The children are
rude and badly-behaved and she does not
seem to have any control over them. They stay
up late watching television, spend far too
much of my money that I send their mother
and seem to be doing pretty badly at school. If I
mention any of this to her, she says I should

have thought about that before I 'ran off'. Is there anything that I can do?

The picture you paint is a gloomy one — and it may be symptomatic of something seriously wrong with both the children and the environment in which they are living. Perhaps their mother simply cannot cope on her own but is unwilling to admit that — especially to you. Try and obtain some indication from the schools about both academic progress and behaviour and attitudes — time-keeping, school activities etc. Then you can consider applying to the court to vary the custody order. Of course if you want to have the children to live with you it will be essential for **you** to be able to show that you can manage to look after them, take them to and from school, deal with illness, holidays and all the hundred and one problems that the daily care of children brings. You could ask the court to appoint a welfare officer to look into the children's well-being, education and home life and then, if the report confirms what you say and fear, the court may direct what is to happen to the children. The court always has the best interests of the children at heart when making any decision.

12 **After our divorce five years ago, our children were left with their mother. They are a boy aged thirteen and a girl of ten. My son says he wants to come and live with me and my second wife. There is nothing we would like better. We live quite near to his mother's house and he would be able to go to the same school and keep the same friends and hobbies. She is totally against the idea and says that a boy 'needs his mother'. What would the court think about this change and would it take any notice of the boy's own wishes?**

The court always starts by asking what is in the child's best interests. Then it looks at the surrounding circumstances of each parent and the practical

arrangements that a change would necessitate. There is
much to be said for teenage boys having the more
direct influence of a father than by mere access.
Certainly the court would take a great deal of notice of
what the boy himself wants — and the reasons for
those wishes. But it strives to be fair to each parent, by
trying to make them both understand that it is the **child**
that is important — not the pride or hurtful motives of
one or other parent.

13 Our marriage is in a pretty bad way — it has
been for years. I have now met someone else
and would like to leave my wife and try again.
The trouble is that I don't think I could afford
to get a divorce. We have three children aged
ten, eight and seven so my wife would have to
keep the house and it would be difficult for her
to work full time. Is there any rough guide to
how much I would be expected to pay in
maintenance?

The first thing you **have** to realise is that it is
impossible for **two** homes to be maintained at a high
standard of living on **one** person's pay. That means that
you, your wife and the children would inevitably feel
the pinch. As for the financial upkeep — you would
have to maintain your wife while she was unable to
work (but not if she **could** work but refused to do so);
and you have to support the children until they
complete their full time education.

For the wife there is no fixed sum — but a rule of
thumb is that she can expect about one-third of the
joint incomes. For example:

Husband's pay (before deductions)	12,000
Wife's part time pay (gross)	2,000
Joint incomes	14,000
One-third of this equals	4,666
Deduct wife's income	2,000

You have to pay your wife

Of course, as you may well be paying the mortgage
on the house (or the rent) this may be taken into
account and affect the sum actually payable to her. For
the children the 'going rate' depends on their age and
needs — but £20 to £30 per week per child is not
uncommon. Remember to take into account that your
wife will be in receipt of Child Benefit for the children
— and this should go to into the calculations.

14 My husband left me; I do work but don't earn
enough to support myself and the children.
Am I entitled to claim from him?

For yourself, you have to apply the 'one-third of joint
earnings' rule (as previously stated in Question 13). But
a father always has to maintain his children — and to
contribute towards the cost of a roof over their heads.
So unless he is unemployed or in prison, in which case
you can seek help from the DHSS — you should ask
him for money for the children, and take him to court if
he refuses.

15 My husband is always late with maintenance.
He is now about two months in arrears and I
am almost penniless. Is there any way I can
make him pay up on time?

Is he employed? If so it is worth registering the divorce
court order for maintenance in the magistrates court
(your solicitor will do that very quickly); then the
money can be collected from his employers via an
'attachment of earnings order'; and if he is in arrears
you can apply to the court for him to be sent to prison if
he does not clear the arrears. The trouble is that should
that be done, the debt is wiped out — so that you lose.
In this case you should go to the DHSS for help. If your
spouse is not employed, you can only use the threat of
prison for non-payment though you might still register
the order in the magistrates court.

16 My wife has walked out leaving me with our two young children and I have given up work to look after them. She has a full time job — can I claim maintenance from her?

In theory — yes. The legislation makes no distinction between those entitled to ask the court for financial orders against a former spouse. If you are forced to give up work to take on the daily care of the children (so placing yourself in the position of many wives staying at home) it seems quite fair that you should be able to get at least some money from your wife to support you and the children.

17 After 30 years of marriage my husband just walked out on me saying he had fallen in love with a woman at work. I have given him and our children (now grown up) the best years of my life. He now says he wants a divorce, that he will sell our lovely home and that I must have something smaller — and support myself. I cannot possibly find work at my age — and there are no jobs here anyway. Why should I be treated in this way?

It is impossible not to feel sorry for people in your position — for the future can look bleak. First — is the house in **his** name only? If so, you can stop a sale 'over your head' by registering a 'land charge' or a 'notice' at one of the departments of the Land Registry. Either ask the Registry to send you details of what to do — or see your solicitor straight away. Secondly, you cannot be forced to divorce him. If you take no action, he will have to wait five years before he can get a divorce himself. See a solicitor and protect your house; he will also advise you about the money side; then sit tight and let your erring husband make the running — and incur the costs. This may well make him see the reality of his present situation — and bring home to him his obligations to **you**.

18 After a very unhappy first marriage I got divorced two years ago. We had a son who was two at the time but his father never showed any interest in him. Since the divorce he has not sent any money for him; he has only seen the boy twice and this year forgot his birthday. I have now met this really nice man and want to marry him. He loves my son and would like to adopt him as his own. Is this possible?

It is not as simple as it looks. First you have to get the court to see whether the boy's future is best dealt with by a custody order rather than adoption. You see, if he was adopted, his natural father would be cut off for good — and though he has shown little interest there may be what he thinks are good reasons for keeping a low profile — until the boy is older, perhaps. If it is decided that you can try for adoption, an independent person is appointed by the court to look at it from all angles — including the boy's point of view. That welfare officer may report either for or against — the court is almost bound to follow that advice. Go and see the solicitor who acted for you when you were divorced and the present custody order was made and ask his advice on the best way forward. Wait until you have re-married and see if **that** works out before you make any decision about adoption.

19 My son is divorced and his two sons seem to spend most of their time with their mother and her family. Certainly she never gets in touch with me and always finds reasons why the boys should not come and see me. Has a grand-parent any legal standing?

If a custody order has been made — which seems likely as the couple are divorced — you, as a grand-parent, may apply for access. Before taking that step, try asking your son to bring the children round.

20 My girlfriend and I are moving into a flat together. We are buying it on a mortgage but do not want to get married. What are our legal rights and should we have a 'contract'?

As far as the flat is concerned, it should be bought in your joint names. At the **outset** you should ensure that the document transferring the flat to you sets out that you are intending to hold it 'on trust for each other as tenants-in-common' in whatever shares you agree **now**. This can be vital because there have been a number of decisions giving little or nothing to women, in particular, when there has been no express 'trust' created. The building society may well want you to create such a trust as a condition for the mortgage offer. As for your 'rights' regarding the contents, cars, money etc — it depends on what you agree and how you operate while you are living together. Separate bank accounts — but with a joint one for household expenses (mortgage, rates, gas and electricity bills etc) — avoid acrimony, so long as each person actually chips in his/her share each month. Get a good solicitor to act for you when you buy the flat and ask him to explain to you the best way in which **both** of you can be protected should things go wrong.

21 My boy-friend and I have lived together for ten years and we are about to split up. The house is in his name and he has paid most of the bills, though I have stayed at home without working to look after his children (by his former marriage) and two of our own. I have run the house, decorated, gardened — all without question. Can I claim half the proceeds of the house?

It looks as though you are in for an unpleasant shock. In 1984 the Appeal Court decided that a woman who had lived with a married man for 17 years, knowing that he would never marry her, but who bore him two children and ran the house was not entitled to claim

any part of the proceeds of the house which he had
bought in his own name. As there was no contribution
in **money** by the woman and no agreement at the time
of purchase about the woman having any beneficial
interest in the house, there was a legal presumption
that the man was the sole owner. To get a share, the
woman would have had to have made a 'substantial'
financial contribution. 'Merely' running the house,
having children and buying furniture and things could
not be called a 'contribution'. Monstrous, you may
think — but the moral is that you should get the legal
ownership tied up at the **outset** of any relationship.
And women should be on their guard if the love of
their life is unwilling to agree to the creation of a 'trust'
for them both.

22 How do you make a will? Do you have to go to a solicitor?

A will is made by writing out carefully and clearly who
is to be the executor and what you want to happen to
your goods and chattels when you die. You date the
will and sign it in the presence of two witnesses who
then also sign it in your presence, and in the presence
of each other. If you have any doubts about what you
want to achieve then you should see a solicitor and get
him to advise you and draw up the will. But about one
third of wills admitted to probate are handwritten.

23 What is so important about signing a will and having witnesses and what happens if they die before you do; does this make the will invalid? And can witnesses benefit under your will?

Making a will avoids complications after you are dead;
it means that your money etc goes to the people **you**
want to benefit. There are strict rules about what
happens when a person dies without making a will —
which means that your millions may go to someone
whom you had no intention of enriching (like the
Crown). And if there is some error in the way in which

your otherwise perfectly satisfactory will is signed and witnessed — you will be treated as **not** having made a will.

When you have set out clearly and unambiguously what you want to happen, the will must be dated and signed by you. Your signature must then be witnessed by **two** people who both sign in your presence, **and** in the presence of each other. And the wording at the foot of the will must make it plain that this is what happened for example: 'Signed by XYZ in our presence and then by us in his and in the presence of each other'.

It does not matter if the witnesses die before you; it does not make the will invalid; it just makes it tidier if there is a problem about the signing (or 'execution') of the will.

Finally — witnesses can **never** benefit under a will; neither can their spouses.

24 What happens to your property if you die without having bothered to make a will?

This is called an 'intestacy'. The division of your wordly goods depends on whether or not you were married, had children or close relatives.

All debts and funeral expenses are paid. What is left is called the net estate. These are some examples:-

(a) you leave a widow and children. The widow gets the personal effects, the first £40,000; what is left is divided in two. She gets a life interest in half (that means the interest); the other half is held for the children until they are 18.

(b) you leave a widow, no children, but your parents are still alive. The widow gets the personal effects, the first £85,000; what is left is divided in two. She gets half; the other half goes directly to the parents.

(c) you leave no widow but several children. Everything goes to the children equally (and is held for any who are under 18).

If you leave neither widow nor children, there is a list of reasonably close relatives who inherit. Broadly, the order is: Parents; brothers/sisters; grand-parents; uncles/aunts; cousins.

If you have none of these — it all goes to the Crown. So you will see that the widow will not automatically get the house if it is in your name — but only a chunk of it — which means it may have to be sold. All very good reasons for ensuring not only that you make a will but that everything is in joint-names as well.

25 What happens if someone dies, no will is found and their affairs are wound up, then later on a will turns up?

It depends. If someone has applied for 'letters of administration' because of the lack of a will (that is an 'intestacy') and has actually done all that is required and has completed the winding up of the dead person's estate — that is that. It is not necessary or possible to recall all the money from the people who received it in good faith. But if the administration is still going on (and it can often take over a year) the personal representative should apply to the probate court to 'revoke' the grant of letters of administration and start all over again according to the will. The chap who was personal representative is entitled to be repaid any out of pocket expenses.

26 I am not married to the man I live with. He won't make a will or give me a share in his house where we have lived together for five years. He has two children that I look after as my own. Have I any rights if he dies?

As far as the house is concerned, not directly (see question 21). But if you are 'dependent' on him at the time of his death, there is scope for you to go to the court and ask for provision to be made for you out of his estate. The court has wide powers to award income and capital and to make orders about houses — so you could be given the right to stay in the house for a time,

say, until you re-married — as well as being given
something to live on. It depends how much money
there is, of course, and what his other financial
obligations might be.

27 I have just re-married at the age of 60. My son
keeps on at me to make a will. I tell him that if
my new husband (who is 65) dies before me,
my son will get it all anyway. I don't want to
waste money on lawyers fees.

How can you be so certain that you will out-live your
new delight? If you are run over by a bus tomorrow,
without making a will, your spouse will get the first
£40,000 of your estate and a life interest in half the rest.
If your total worth is small — your son may not get very
much — if anything. So, if you want your lad to benefit
— make a will. Of course, you may not want him to —-
money grabbing little so-and-so! But making a will to
leave it all to your new husband or to the dogs' home
saves problems.

28 My husband was killed in a traffic accident.
The house was in his name and though his
firm have been very good, the money is
running out. I have two children aged seven
and ten and need all the cash I can get. The
solicitor who is dealing with the probate says I
won't get all that my husband left. Surely a
widow with children to bring up is entitled to
all her husband's property.

It looks as though your husband died 'intestate' —
without a will. In that case the rules about who gets
what (as set out in Question 24) come into operation.
You will get your husband's personal effects — car,
furniture etc; and the first £40,000 of his money; the
rest is split in two parts. You get a life interest in half;
the other half is held until the children are 18.

29 I have been having an affair for over 30 years. The man sees me every fortnight and gives me money on which I live. He also pays bills for the house and for holidays. If he dies I shall have no money at all as I have always relied on what he gives me. Would I have any claim on his estate?

Yes you will — if you can establish 'dependency' and there is enough money in his estate to be able to provide for you. It is important that you make enquiries immediately he dies — because your right to financial help has to be applied for within six months of probate being granted. Don't hang about waiting for someone to contact **you**.

30 I am happily married to the best husband in the world. All our property — house, bank account, savings etc — are in both our names. If either of us die, would we need to bother with probate?

Probably not, so long as literally everything is in joint names and the intention is that the survivor should take the lot when one of you dies. For the avoidance of doubt there is no harm in making a simple will leaving 'everything that I own' to your husband. And what happens if you died together in a crash? You really ought to make a proper provision to ensure that the right people get what you have so thriftily accumulated. Why not see your solicitor about this?

31 What is an 'executor' and is it true that they can't benefit from a will?

An executor's task is to collect all your assets, pay the bills, funeral expenses and tax and then distribute what is left according to the will. He can employ a solicitor to help him do this (indeed it is not uncommon to appoint your solicitor to be the executor). Certainly he **can** benefit; it's only witnesses who can't. Once upon a

time, one used to leave a sum of money to one's
executor to reward him for taking on the chore. It is
important to make sure that any person whom you
would like to act as executor is actually willing to do
so. And that he is likely to outlive you.

32 I am 23 and expecting a baby. I know who the
father is but there is no chance of any
permanent relationship. Indeed, neither of us
want that. Do I have to tell the hospital who
the father is or put his name on the birth
certificate? And will he have any rights after
the baby is born?

The starting point is that for illegitimate births the
father's name is **not** normally noted. But there are
several ways in which his name may be put on the
birth certificate:
  (a) by both of you applying and asking the registrar
      to do so;
  (b) by doing it along with a declaration by you that
      he is the father and a declaration by him
      acknowledging fatherhood; or
  (c) by producing a copy of an affiliation order in
      which he is named as the father.
  As to your last point, he can apply to the court for
custody — or ask to be made party to any proceedings
started by you or any other person.

33 I have been living with a man for almost 30
years. Everyone thinks we are married but the
problem is he is a Catholic and won't divorce
his wife. We want to make wills leaving
everything to each other and our accountant is
devising a scheme to defeat capital transfer
tax, based on our being married. What can we
do? We have no children.

You **must** come clean with your accountant. I bet he
has been claiming married man's tax allowance over
the years. Why do you not get married now? A divorce
can be done very simply without fuss or publicity.

Then you would not be deceiving anyone. By doing so, you will also save a very large amount of capital transfer tax (or the new inheritance tax) because all gifts from husband to wife (and vice versa) are exempt from **all** tax on death.

34 My daughter who is 14 wants to earn some pocket-money. Is it legal for her to have a job?

The general rule is tht no child can be employed:

- so long as he is under 13;
- before school closing time;
- before 7 am and after 7 pm;
- for more than two hours on a school day or a Sunday.

But there may be local regulations or by-laws in force permitting not more than one hour's work before school. Check with your local council to see if such an order has been made.

35
My children are ten and thirteen and are both sensible enough to be left alone while my husband and I go out for the evening. Is it legal for them to be left on their own in this way for a few hours?

Probably yes — there is no specific criminal offence of going out for the night leaving the kids at home. But it **is** an offence to leave a child under twelve in a room with an unprotected open fire or heating appliance in case the child is injured or killed. So leave them in the cold! Seriously, one has to take reasonable steps to ensure the safety of one's children. And much will depend on the degree of responsibility which the older child may have.

36
I want to change my surname from Smith to Jones. People at work are saying that I shall need my former husband's agreement (we are not divorced but have lived apart for years) and will have to get a deed poll whatever that may be. Is there an easier way?

Yes. You make a simple statutory declaration saying 'I was for years known as Rosemary Smith and from now on I wish to be known as Rosemary Jones'. You date this and sign it and take it to a solicitor or commissioner for oaths. He will take £3 from you and Bob's your uncle. This will be accepted by the Passport Office, DHSS, Banks — most people who need an 'official' change of name document. You don't need the consent of your former husband. You don't even have to tell him. If you had wanted a Deed Poll (which is a very formal document needing to be enrolled in the Royal Courts of Justice) it would have been expensive and his consent **would** have been required.

37
When I was 15 my 'parents' told me I was adopted. Since then I have wanted to find out who my real parents are. Have I any legal rights now that I am 18 — and how do I go about it?

You are entitled to ask the Registrar General to supply you with information to enable you to obtain your 'real' birth certificate. The Registrar is under a duty to tell you about counselling services — either at the General Register Office or by a local authority or the adoption agency which placed you. And you should take advantage of this **before** you get a copy of your original birth certificate. While you may well want to know your origins, you must also think about how your natural parents might feel about your descending out of the blue.

38 Apart from 'coming of age' at 18 — what are the limits at which children can do things nowadays, like driving and buying drink?

Here are some of the most sought after:

Age	Activity
12	Buy pet animals

14	Go into a public house (but **not** buy or consume alcohol) Pledge goods in a pawnshop
16	Buy fireworks/buy cigarettes and tobacco Get married (so long as parents consent)
17	Drive a car and motorbike Have an airgun in a public place Take part in street trading
18	Marry without parents' consent Vote Buy alcohol in a public house or off-licence Enter a betting shop Buy houses

39 I want to go away on holiday for a fortnight in June — which is during term-time. My children's head-teacher says that she will not allow them leave of absence. Is she right?

No. It is perfectly proper and legal for a parent to take a child from school for up to two weeks in term-time. Obviously if the child is doing exams it would be daft — but legally the teacher cannot object.

Accidents etc

1 I fell off a pair of step-ladders while redecorating and broke my leg. The ladder had seemed a bit wonky and though I can't remember what actually happened I seem to recall that the steps suddenly 'opened' as if the rope which joined them had broken. I have been off work for several months; what are my legal rights?

There are two possible claims open to you to explore. First — did **you** buy the steps? And if so, was it within the last few months? If the answer to both these questions is 'yes' — then you may well have a claim against the shop that sold the ladder because it was not of 'merchantable quality' nor 'fit for its intended use' (see Shopping section). Of course you have to show that your injury arose because of a defect in the ladder and not because you lost your balance or were over-loading the ladder.

  If you did not buy the ladder yourself — the only chance is to be able to show that someone — usually the manufacturers — was 'negligent'. To succeed in this sort of claim you need technical evidence to explain how the ladder was designed and constructed and in what way it was defective — and that it was reasonably foreseeable by the manufacturer of the ladder that the defect might lead to injury. So, if the rope was not strong enough to take the strain of a person who was above average weight, for example, you might have a claim. You must therefore have kept the evidence — that is, the ladder. This sort of legal action is not easy but it is worth getting legal advice at an early stage — if only to be told that there is no chance of success.

2 My ten year old was out on his bike riding along the pavement (as the road traffic is so heavy). He ran into an elderly neighbour, knocking her over and breaking her glasses. I felt morally obliged to help her, but am I legally bound?

It depends why your lad was riding his bike. If you had
sent him to the shop to buy your evening paper, he
would have been acting as your 'agent' — and you
would be liable to meet any claim for damages brought
against him. But if he was just out playing — 'on a
frolic of his own' as a judge once put — then he, and
only he, is liable. Of course you may have public
liability insurance covering the whole family which
may meet the point.

3   **While decorating our upstairs outside window
frame, the painter rested his foot (and put his
weight) on the window ledge. The ledge
eventually gave way and the painter fell,
breaking his leg. He is saying that he can claim
compensation from us for loss of earnings, as
the ledge was rotten and it's therefore our fault
that he fell. I say he should not have put his
weight on the ledge as he should have realised
it wouldn't be strong enough. He had a ladder
anyway! Who is right?**

Both of you in a way. The law says that the owner of a
house should ensure that the premises will be
reasonably safe for the purposes for which a visitor
comes to the house. So there is an onus on you to make
sure that the 'public' parts of your property — the
drive, doorways, floors, staircases and electrical
systems are **reasonably** safe. On the other hand, the
same law says that you may expect a tradesman (like a
painter, window-cleaner or plumber for example) to
appreciate **and** guard against any special risks which
are connected with his job, so long as you leave him
free to do so. So if he was fool enough to stand on the
window ledge knowing that these things are not
designed for that purpose — he took a chance. It would
be different if you had been standing in the drive
telling him to do so. He has no claim against you.

   Moral: All self-employed people should think very
hard about insurance against loss of income through
injury.

4   A visitor to my house tripped over a loose
        carpet in my hall and twisted his knee. He has
        lost a month's pay and says I should
        compensate him. Surely this cannot be right?

Well, you owe him a duty of care to ensure that your
house is reasonably safe. So if the carpet was loose,
and you knew it was, and failed either to nail it down,
rope it off, or warn visitors, then you may well be
liable. Look at the public liability clause in your
household and/or buildings insurance policy. You
may find that your insurers will meet this sort of claim.

5   Someone slipped and fell on the ice on the
        pavement outside my front gate. I have been
        told that it is my fault as each house-holder is
        responsible for the path in front of their house.
        Is this true?

There is a lot of hot air talked about snow. You may be
liable if you sweep snow into piles on the **road**; if you

allow accumulations of snow hanging over the roof to fall into the street; if you sweep the snow off the footpath and then pour on boiling water (to get rid of the ice) but which freezes and makes things worse. But, unless there are by-laws in force in your district, there is no general duty for house-holders to clean pavements or footpaths (unlike in many countries in Europe). There is a duty on the highway authority to remove obstructions arising on the road from the accumulation of snow. If they fail to do so, anyone may make a complaint to a magistrates court. And the council may face a compensation claim — there was a case in 1984 where a girl slipped on packed snow and ice which had lain on a pavement for four to six weeks.

6 **I slipped on a greasy floor in a local supermarket and hurt my arm. When I complained the manager said that another customer had spilled something and I should have looked where I was going. Have I a claim?**

Shops must ensure that their floors and entrances are kept clean, well-lit and safe. Of course in a supermarket people will drop things and make a mess. What the shop has to do — to avoid paying compensation to a customer who is injured because of the mess — is to have a proper system for regular inspection and clearing up. In one case where a customer had slipped on some yogurt, it was shown that the store had no properly organised system and that over 15 minutes had passed before anyone bothered to come round with a mop. So if you can show that the greasy mess had been on the floor for some time without anyone in the shop attempting to clear it up — you will have a claim.

7 **While I was driving along a motorway, a wheel came off my car and there was a crash. The car was 18 months old (had done 15,000 miles) and the garage which had just serviced it said that it was 'one of those things'.**

Surely someone must be to blame and should compensate me?

It's the old story about 'evidence' again. What caused the wheel to come off? Was the axle defective; the metal fatigued; the nuts not properly tightened; had you hit a kerbstone or lump of concrete lying on the road? In order to get any legal claim off the ground you **must** get technical evidence from an engineer who is prepared to go into the witness box and say that he has been looking at wheels man and boy for 30 years and that the reason for this incident was ... whatever it was. Without that you have a virtually impossible task and may just have to rely on your insurers to pay you a fair price for the written off car.

8 **Walking on the kerb trying to cross the road, I was hit by the wing mirror of a passing car. The driver said it was my fault for standing so close to the road. Is he right?**

No he is not. He has to use the road sensibly, and that means he takes notice of pedestrians on the pavement and approaching the road. So he should not drive too close and should also be aware that his mirror sticks out. If you lost pay or were injured — you have a claim against him.

9 **What does one have to do as a motorist if there is an accident?**

If there is an 'accident' (which is defined as causing death, personal injury or damage to **any** property like another vehicle, a garden wall, a tree etc) and you were one of the drivers involved:
- you **must** stop
- you must give your name and address to anyone with reasonable grounds for wanting it (like a victim or the owner of the property which has been damaged)
- if someone has been injured you must give him

details of your insurance
- if you don't give anyone your name and address (and insurance details in an injury case) you **must as soon as possible** and within 24 hours report the accident to the police and produce your driving licence, MOT certificate (if relevant) and insurance particulars.

10 I have an evening job. While loading a lorry with boxes I stepped back and fell to the ground. I was seriously injured. When I tried to make a claim, a man from the firm's insurance company said that as I was 'moonlighting' I had no legal rights at all. After six months in hospital I am anxious to try and get back some of my lost pay. Is there anything I can do?

Yes. Sue the firm for damages for personal injury. They failed to provide you with a 'safe system of working' because they allowed you to climb on the back of a lorry to unload it without any sort of safety device. The fact that you were working at a different place from your day job is completely irrelevant. See a solicitor — or ask the hospital social worker to find one who will visit you in hospital and act for you while you are still away from home.

11 I was recently involved in an accident in which my car was badly damaged. The accident was not my fault and I have witnesses to prove that. However the other driver drove off immediately; no-one got his number. The police cannot trace him. If I claim on my own insurance I will lose my no claims bonus. Is this fair?

No — but it is the way life is. That is why you have insurance to protect you (and others) in the event that you cannot get compensation from anyone else.

12 A man drove into the side of my car. He admits that it was his fault but refuses to tell me the name of his insurers. Whan can I do?

If there was no injury he does not have to give you insurance details. But your remedy is to sue **him** for the loss which you sustained. That may well make him go to his insurance company. On the other hand, if he is self-employed, unemployed or with 'no fixed abode' think hard before spending good money on taking him to court; you may win but still not get your money.

13 I swerved to avoid hitting a small child who ran into the road in front of my car, and I hit a lamp-post. Is the child's parent liable for the cost of repairing my car?

Not unless he bodily threw the child into the road. You take other road users as you find them and must keep a look out for children, dogs, cats as well as other vehicles which act unpredictably.

14 What happens if you are in an accident and the guilty driver is driving a stolen car?

You have a good claim against the thief. Whether you will actually get any money is another matter, of course, because people who steal cars are less likely to be willing to pay damages to their victims. If you were injured, and the thief was uninsured (which seems extremely probable) you may be able to resort to the Motor Insurers Bureau. This is a scheme run by the insurance industry to provide compensation for the victims of 'hit and run' drivers. It **only** operates where a person is killed or injured — **not** for damage to cars or property.

15 I was standing in a bus going to work when the driver slammed on the brakes and I was thrown to the floor, spraining my wrist. The police were called but the driver said he had to stop because a dog had run into the road. Surely that was his problem and he can't get out of compensating me and the other passengers who were injured.

He is only liable if he was 'negligent' — that is, it was he who was to blame for the accident. He wasn't. The dog was. You may have a legal claim against the owner of the dog for failing to keep it under control — but the driver acted reasonably.

16 My husband works for a firm who make chemicals. They provide safety-wear which seems inadequate. Recently he was working with strong chemicals which burned him badly. He was wearing a safety suit but when he looked at it afterwards there was a small tear. The firm says he should have examined it before wearing it or that he tore it through carelessness. My husband says he was not careless — and, anyway, surely it's the firm's responsiblity to check the clothing?

Employers have to make the workplace as safe as it can reasonably be — taking into account that dangerous materials are used. So they have to provide proper safety clothing and equipment. Obviously, even in the best run places accidents will happen — so it is just possible that your husband **did** damage the suit himself even though he may not have realised. You can argue that the firm ought to have stronger safety suits which would not tear. Has your husband seen his trade union representative? There may well be the makings of a claim which can often be best processed via the union as they have the experience and the specialist knowledge. If not, your husband should see a solicitor.

17 I work on a farm. I injured an arm when a barn door swung back suddenly. Previously I had told the farmer that the door was faulty. He says that as I cannot lift anything and my arm hurts I will have to get another job. Surely he owes me something?

Do you belong to the TGWU? Their Agricultural section should be able to help you. If not, see a solicitor immediately. If the door was known to be unsafe, you will have a claim against the farmer for damages for the injury and if he sacks you, for wrongful dismissal as well.

18 My brother was involved in an accident while cycling to work. A lorry turned left across his path without indicating. As a result, my brother has been badly injured. He will be permanently disabled and won't be able to go mountaineering or cycling again. The police say that they are not going to prosecute the driver. Does this mean my brother has no claim for compensation?

Not at all. There are many reasons why drivers are not prosecuted in the criminal courts after an accident. That must not be confused with bringing a **civil** claim for 'damages' for injuries. Of course it strengthens your case if you show that the driver **was** convicted in a magistrates court for driving without due care and attention. But the lack of any criminal prosecution does

not stop you. Your brother is entitled not to be driven into by lorries while lawfully cycling along the road.

He may well have a strong claim — he should see a solicitor now and gather as much evidence from witnesses as quickly as possible.

19 Why is it that compensation for injury seems to be a lottery depending on random factors — like how you were injured or who caused it, rather than based on your actual *needs?*

It's because our system is based on a claim being successful if, and only if, you can prove that someone was to **blame**. Imagine three people lying next to each other in hospital with broken legs. One fell off a ladder at home while cleaning his gutters — he will probably get nothing. The next was injured at work — his prospects are very good as his employers will almost certainly have to compensate him because they failed to provide a safe system of working. The third person was run over on a zebra crossing. He will probably be fully compensated. In some countries — New Zealand, for example — there is a state run 'no-fault' scheme for accident compensation. There, you get a proportion of your pre-accident earnings until you are better and are given facilities for rehabilitation; though you may receive a much smaller lump sum than is paid here. Their system is based wholly on **need**; blame does not come into the equation at all. Until our legal system is completely changed and the concept of 'no-fault' liability is introduced, the present lottery will continue.

20 I was injured in a car crash some years ago. After a lot of difficulty the driver's insurance company offered my solicitor a sum of money in settlement of the claim. Reluctantly I accepted in order to avoid having to go to court. Now there are problems as a consequence of the injuries I received. My back is giving me constant pain and I find it difficult to sleep except for short periods.

Is there any way I can re-open the case and try to get more compensation?

No. The payment you were offered and accepted was in 'full and final settlement' of your claim for compensation. Even if you had declined that money and gone to court (where you might have got more or less) the award by the court is a final one. The intention is to enable those who have to pay out to be certain that once they have done so there will be no come-back in the future. So long as the existing system is retained, that seems to be the fairest way of striking a balance between the competing interests.

There is a new system whereby an injured person can apply to the court for 'provisional damages' ' which may enable him to go back to court if his condition deteriorates. It will be interesting to see how this works.

21 While I was driving into a municipal car park, the arm of the barrier suddenly dropped onto the windscreen of my car doing £1000 worth of damage. The council says it was because of vandalism and they won't pay my bill. Are they right?

Almost certainly yes. So long as they have a regular and reasonable system of inspecting and maintaining equipment, they will not be liable if vandals do their worst. You cannot expect them to place a man on every automatic barrier just in case a group of yobs roll up and break it. You should ask to see the detailed records of the council's inspection of this machine and the barrier. If they can't or won't produce this, then it may be because there **isn't** one — or that it exists but shows that they have not done their job properly. Get your solicitor to ask for the records and then to consider making a claim for you.

22 My neighbour has complained that my cat has been in his garden and dug up some seedlings.

He wants me to pay for the damage which the cat has done. Do I have to?

Fortunately for cat owners, there is no liability for what they get up to. Unlike dogs (which are supposed to be controllable) cats are recognised as having minds of their own; and can do what they want where and when they want — without any human being responsible.

23 Recently I had a carpet fitted in a room which had been decorated. The fitters completely ruined some of the paintwork on the skirting boards. I think they should pay for this to be put right — but they say there is a clause in their contract which says they are not liable for any accidental damage. Is this right?

When a tradesman does any work, there is a legal implication that he will do whatever has to be done to the standard of a reasonably competent member of his

trade or calling. So if the carpet fitters have mucked up
the paint work — they are in breach of their contract.
The clause in their contract will only allow them to
avoid this responsibility if, and only if, it is held by a
court to be fair and reasonable. And the law says that
the onus of showing that it **is** fair rests on the trader. So
he would have to go into the witness box and justify his
attempt to get out of his legal duty. So tell the fitters to
pay for the work or else . . . sue.

24 My aunt recently had a simple eye operation.
She subsequently had continuous pain and
discomfort, and now has to go back to the
hospital for further surgery. She suspects the
operation was not done properly in the first
place. Should she seek a second opinion with a
view to a claim?

Yes. The only chance at all of being successful in a
claim against a doctor is to get at least one other
medical expert to be prepared to go into the box and
say that his colleague was negligent. Not easy to find.

25 Last spring while playing football I was
heavily tackled by an opponent and broke a
leg. The man was 'booked' by the referee. Do I
have any rights?

Nasty rough game, football. Nevertheless, it should be
played in a sporting and fair way within the rules. And
if a player steps outside the bounds of fairness —
especially in a contact sport — and **deliberately** causes
injury, he can be sued and ordered to compensate his
victim. You have to prove that the tackle was unfair
and the 'booking' is some support. You will probably
have to get the referee to give evidence.

26 What is the difference between 'assault' and
'battery'?

'Assault' is the action of putting someone in fear of
being struck. There is no need to use violence; it is

enough if the victim has reasonable grounds for
believing that he is in danger of it. So it is an assault to
shake a fist in someone's face or to point a gun at
someone. 'Battery' is the consequence of an intentional
assault — which brings some object into contact with
the victim. Throwing water over a person; or pulling a
chair from under someone so that he falls to the
ground; snatching a bag or garment; all these are
examples of battery. 'Assault' needs fear; 'battery' a
blow. Anyone can bring a civil claim for damages for
assault, although as most assaults end in contact, the
claim is strictly for battery. While there is a let out for
the sort of trivial contact needed to draw a person's
attention to something, and for the person who is a
jolly 'back-slapper', the law can take a serious view of
this type of conduct. Don't feel free to kiss a pretty girl
or boy as they pass you by. It may not be assault
because the victim would not be in fear — but it's
certainly battery and you can be sued.

27 When I went to the loo at a restaurant I took
off my rings. I only realised this when I got
home — and needless to say nobody at the
restaurant has any knowledge of the rings,
which have disappeared. Surely the place
should have been covered by insurance?

The rings were yours; why did you take them off — and
why did you not remember them? It seems
unreasonable to expect someone else to compensate
you for your own misfortune. A prudent person would
have an 'all risks' extension to the household insurance
policy — which would enable you to make a claim
against your insurers.

28 I returned from a winter holiday to discover
that a burst pipe had caused considerable
damage to the carpets and decoration in my
bungalow. I am having problems getting the
insurance company to pay because they say I
should have left the heating on — or drained
down the system. I did neither. I have often

taken winter holidays without taking such
precautions. Surely they should pay up
without such fuss?

Most insurance policies do not require systems to be
drained down unless the house is to be empty for a
long period — a month or more. So — what is the
actual wording in your policy? Read it and see if there
is a specific direction that the tank etc should be
drained. If there is, then the insurer may well be acting
correctly in turning down your claim. If not — pursue
the matter with the Chief General Manager of the
company. Of course if there was a very cold spell when
you went away and you failed to take precautions
against that, you may have contributed to the situation
and be unable to make a claim.

29 Is it really necessary to read all the 'small print' on an insurance form? Surely they all say much the same?

Not at all. That is why there is so much competition by insurance companies. You should always get hold of as much detail as possible of the terms and conditions of an insurance policy **before** you actually enter into a contract. And, above all, you should note what is **not** included or is specifically **excluded** from the cover. Too often people only read the policy **after** something has happened and discover that they are not covered for something that they thought they had been paying for.

30 My daughter lives in a rented bed-sit in a large house which contains six other flatlets. Who should take out the insurance — my daughter or the landlord?

It is the landlord's responsibility to insure the building itself — the bricks and mortar — against fire, and your daughter would do well to ask to see a copy of the current insurance certificate. It is not unknown for landlords to have inadequate (or non-existent) insurance. For her own things, you daughter should have a home contents policy and, of course, should explain in detail to the insurance company that she lives in a bed-sit, because that may affect the premium rate.

31 Our house was recently burgled. The insurance people were very good but I was amazed to discover that, although we were fully insured, we only got back the market value of what was stolen and not their replacement value. Our TV and stereo cassette player were both five years old but they will cost very much more to replace than the insurers gave us.

You only get the actual value of something which is damaged or destroyed unless you specifically insure for replacement value. This naturally increases the premium payable — which is why many people take out the lesser cover.

32 One of the teachers at my son's school drove
    my son and two other boys in his car to a
    nearby school for a football match. I didn't say
    anything at the time — but would the teacher's
    insurance have covered any accident?

Almost certainly yes. But — it depends whether the
teacher has any limitation on the use of the car. If he
can only use it for 'social, domestic and pleasure'
purposes he might **not** be covered because it is
arguable that taking the lads to football was part of his
employment, and that he was therefore using the car
for business purposes. If you want to be certain, ask the
teacher to confirm to you (in writing if possible) that
the insurance cover is sufficiently comprehensive to
extend to this sort of event. If he can't (or won't) then I
think you should have a word with the head teacher
and explain why you are unwilling for your son to
travel in this way.

33 I often see signs in public places saying that
    what is left there is at 'owner's risk'. Even my
    dry-cleaners have a sign saying that they are
    not liable if things go wrong. Surely if I pay to
    put my car in a car park, or my coat in a
    cloakroom, or for my curtains to be cleaned,
    then the people in charge ought to be
    responsible for what happens?

There is nothing illegal about trying to limit one's
liability. But whether that attempt is successful
depends on whether the form of words used is
sufficiently unambiguous and whether the 'exclusion'
is fair or reasonable. The law says that if the wording is
not clear, the worst construction is used. So 'cars
parked at owner's risk' could be said to mean 'at the
risk of owner of the **car-park**! The test of fairness
means that the trader will have to justify his exclusion
of liability. Payment for a service imposes a contractual
obligation on the other side to do the thing properly —
to safeguard your car, or your coat or to clean your

curtains. But a car-park is not responsible if some
stranger bangs into your car. Handing your coat in
makes the people responsible for making sure it is not
handed back to the wrong person. Always make sure
you get a ticket or a receipt proving that they have the
article.

34 Last month we went on holiday. We took a
train from Newcastle to London and were to
fly from Gatwick. Our train was three hours
late and we missed the flight. We got a later
plane, but had to pay over £100 extra to
change flights because the tickets were 'non-
transferable'. It wasn't our fault we missed the
flight; can I claim from British Rail?

Yes. They have a contract with you to run their trains
according to the time-table they publish. Although
they try to exclude their liability for any breach by
saying that they don't guarantee to run according to the
time-table (or at all) you can sue them and leave them
to try and justify their terms and conditions. Having to
pay the extra air fares was 'consequential loss' arising
directly as a result of the failure of BR to meet their
contractual obligation.

35 My friend had a heart attack while on holiday abroad. I thought he would be covered by the holiday insurance, but the company says it is not liable as my friend did not declare his heart condition on their application form. He says he had been told as a child that he had a weak heart, but had never had trouble and, anyway, there was no relevant question on the form. Can he pursue his claim.

An insurer can only go on what you tell him; you are a stranger to him and so let him have as much information as possible which relates to the risk you are asking him to insure against. Because he knows more about what is important to **him**, he should design his proposal form to indicate to you the things that he wants you to think about and tell him.

For medical/life insurance, a history of a heart condition is obviously very relevant. But if your friend had not given any thought to his 'weak heart' for many years and had lived quite normally without any medical attention — then a reasonable insurer would not think that there had been a deliberate withholding of vital details and would pay up. Write to the Chief General Manager of the company explaining that it is being unfair and if need be consider suing (or at least getting a solicitor to write to the company).

36 I was knocked over while on a Zebra Crossing. Have I any claim against the driver?

The law says that any driver must be able to stop in the event of any conceivable use of a crossing by any conceivable pedestrian, other than a suicide. So you **always** get some compensation against a motorist who hits you on a zebra — though if you acted foolishly by stepping out at the last minute, when he could not stop, your damages may be reduced.

37

I was about to get on a train which was standing still at the platform, when it suddenly moved forward about a yard — then stopped again. My hand was on the door handle and I was dragged off balance, injuring myself and ruining my raincoat. Have I got a claim against the railways?

Yes: So long as you can prove that they were negligent. They may have to do things with the train — add locomotives, shunt carriages — which means moving what would otherwise look like a stationary train. In that case, they must make sure that passengers are warned not to go near the train and platform staff should be on hand to supervise. If none of these safeguards were present, you should write to the Area Manager of the Region and set out in detail what happened — giving dates and times — and claiming the cost of whatever you have lost. If your injury means that you are off work and therefore do not yet know exactly how much you are out of pocket — you simply say that you are claiming damages 'to be assessed in due course'. If your claim is not quickly processed or they deny liability, go to a solicitor for help.

38

What is the responsibility of a dog owner should his hound run out into the road?

Owners of dogs have a legal duty to control their animals, and to take reasonable steps to prevent them causing damage to other people lawfully using the highway. So dogs should be kept on a lead; the lead should not be so long as to cause the dog to trip up passers by. And gardens should be sufficiently fenced so that a dog cannot get out and roam on his own. If having taken all these precautions, your dog gets out — you will not be liable because you have acted reasonably. But if you do not bother to observe these simple rules and someone is injured — expect a claim. You can get special 'pet' insurance cover which is worth investigating when you get a puppy.

39 While I was moving house, the removal van
carrying my furniture collided on the road
because the driver of the *other* vehicle
involved had been stung by a wasp (so he
said). Most of my stuff was ruined. What is my
position?

It was not the fault of the removal van driver; so there is
no claim for 'negligence' against that firm. If the other
man **was** stung — then he was not negligent either.
Your only claim is against the removal firm for breach
of contract — because they could not do what they had
promised to do; or under their insurance policy —
assuming you had paid the additional fee for full cover.
If not — you may simply have no claim against anyone.

40 Is there any time limit for making a claim for
injuries? My brother was injured at work
about three years ago and though he went to a
solicitor, nothing much seems to have
happened.

You **must** issue a writ to start proceedings for personal
injury damages not later than three years after the date
of the injury. If you don't you are out of time and have
almost certainly lost your right to go to court. Get your
brother to make certain that a writ **was** issued within
time. If it was not — he should go immediately to a new
solicitor because there will probably be a claim for
negligence against the present firm.

41 I have read about tragic cases in which
children have been killed in accidents but
their parents have not been able to get very
much money. Why is this — when you lose
your most cherished possession, surely the
damages should be huge?

Because it is impossible to put a figure on the life of a
child, and to try and avoid anguish for the parents, the
law recently put into statutory form the nominal sum to

be paid to the parents of a child who is killed — and fixed it at £3500. No other money can be claimed — unless the parents can show that they were dependent on the child. This may be possible if the child was adult, unmarried, without children and actually supported his/her parents. But if the child is under 18 this is most unlikely.

42 In a restaurant the waiter tipped red wine over me ruining a new and expensive dress. Have I a claim for cleaning or a replacement?

Almost certainly you do; if the dress is new, your claim is for the actual cost of it. Should you be able to have it cleaned — and it would be reasonable to try that first — the damages equal the cost of cleaning plus travel to and from the cleaners. The only doubt is if the accident was caused by some external and unpreventable cause — like a wasp stinging the waiter, or some clumsy oaf at the next table knocking his arm just at the critical moment. In this case there may be no claim at all, because there would have been no negligence by the waiter. But if he had simply not taken any proper care or concentration the restaurant is liable.

43 I was driving home one afternoon when the road in front of my car suddenly disappeared; smoke from a roadside fire had completely obliterated the view ahead. I lost all sense of direction and hit the kerb, damaging the car and being unable to get home. Apparently some small-holder had decided to burn a pile of rubbish and had overlooked the fact that it was wet and so would smoke. He has shown little interest in my request that he pay the bill. Am I right that I can claim against him?

There are two aspects of this. First, and most important from your point of view, his civil liability. If one lights a fire and allows the smoke to blow across a road, it is obviously foreseeable that passing motorists will be put in danger. So you have a good claim against the man who lit and 'controlled' the fire for damages. If he won't play ball, see a local solicitor and get him to press the matter for you. Secondly, there is the criminal law. Under the Highways Act 1980 it is an offence to light a fire within 50 feet of the centre of a highway with the consequence that traffic is interrupted or road users injured or endangered. This carries a maximum fine on 'Level 3' — which is presently £400. So you can tell the police and ask them to prosecute the man; or you can apply to the magistrates court yourself for a summons. If the fire was lit more than 50 feet away but the man intended that it should spread near the road, it may still be possible for him to be convicted.

44 During a recent thunderstorm I was knocked off my bike by a car. Fortunately I was only grazed but the bike was a write-off. The car driver said that he couldn't see me; I certainly could not see him because he had no lights on. When I asked him why not, he said that he did not want to over-load his battery. Surely there is some law about this?

It's amazing how many drivers still believe that if they

have their lights on when the engine is running, the battery will be getting flat! This is *not* so. Modern cars all have a device which keeps the electrical charge in the battery topped up all the time the engine is running. It is an offence not to have lights on when the visibility is poor or when it's dark, of course. Main or dipped headlights must be kept on while a car or other vehicle is in motion during any period when poor visibility conditions prevail on the road. So if it's raining, or overcast, or the daylight suddenly goes — headlights *must* be switched on.

45 **During the winter a slate fell from my roof and nearly hit a woman on the pavement. I didn't know there was anything wrong with the roof. I can only assume that the bad weather had something to do with it. Have I any legal responsibility?**

Only if it can be shown that you knew or ought reasonably to have known that the roof slates were likely to come off. If you had simply neglected the upkeep, then you may well be liable either for damages for *nuisance;* or, if you had deliberately done nothing, for *negligence*. If you took normal precautions and had the roof looked at from time to time and had no reason to believe that anything was wrong, you would not be responsible if a slate came off. The best thing is to make certain that you have property insurance cover against what is called 'public liability'. Then if this sort of event occurs, any liability on your part would be met by the insurers.

46 **Coming round a corner on a country lane, I hit a cow which was straying on the side of the road. Eventually I traced the owner of the land, who said that he had let it to a cattle breeder. The cow man said that it was not his fault because the field should have been fenced. Who is going to pay the bill?**

Owners of livestock have a duty to ensure that cattle etc

do not stray on to the highway. So *someone* is liable to you; the problem is finding who. It depends on the basis on which the field was let. If there was adequate fencing at the outset but it deteriorated without the land-owner knowing — the cowman would be liable to meet your bill. If there were inadequate fences, or if they were broken down during the letting and the owner knew about it but did not attempt to put them right and make the field stockproof — it's *his* responsiblity.

47 **My seven-year old daughter was playing at school during break and fell in the playground. There is a raised concrete platform (which is thought to have been the base of an old building) and she tripped over this while running. The school referred my claim to an insurance company which said there was no negligence on the part of the school staff — and so no basis for my daughter to be compensated. Surely this is wrong?**

It is true that the Education Authority (via its insurers) will only have to pay if it can be shown that it was negligent. But this covers more than just the supervision by the teachers at the school. It is quite possible for playgrounds to be adequately overseen but for the authority to be negligent. The premises must be reasonably safe for the ordinary purposes of a school; and this would mean that unnecessary obstructions or dangerous bits and pieces should either be removed or be fenced off so that children (and other visitors) cannot be injured. This 'raised platform' seems to be something which the Education Authority has known about for some time and ought to have done something about. Go to a solicitor and get him to take up this aspect of the case with the council's insurers.

Owning or renting a house

1 I put my house on the market. A nice young couple came and saw it; then they made a firm offer which I accepted. The legal work was started. Thinking they were genuine I found a bungalow and was on the point of exchanging contracts when the couple's solicitor told mine they had changed their minds. So everything fell through. I have lost the bungalow and spent a lot of money on searches, a survey and the legal work. Have I any redress against the couple who let me down?

Afraid not. It does seem very unfair, but it is a consequence of the system. There is **no** binding or enforceable deal for the sale and purchase of property **until** contracts are 'exchanged'. Until then any party may withdraw. If your survey on the bungalow had been bad, you would probably have 'let down' the seller of that house by withdrawing. The only way to get a firm, binding commitment is to get to the point of exchange of contracts as quickly as your own situation allows. The trouble is that very few people would wish to be in the position either of owning two houses, which can happen if you exchange contracts on your purchase **before** you sell — or of having no roof over their heads, which will be the result of exchanging contracts on the sale **before** you find a place to buy. Most people need the cash from one house to put towards the next one and also need a mortgage and until it is certain that the money will be there on the right day in the right amount, it is understandable that few people are willing to enter into any financial commitment. And until the deal is binding, each side has to bear its own expenses should it fall through.

2 I have heard a lot about bridging loans. Would this not be a way of coping with the problem?

Only if you are rich, or a gambler with nerves of steel. In reality no financial institution will lend you money

unless it **knows** that you are in a secure position. The commonest form of bridging loan is to cover the deposit which has to be paid on exchange of contracts. But very few people could get a bridging loan to buy a house unless and until they had sold their existing one. For example, just say your present house was worth £40,000; you have a £25,000 mortgage. The new place you are buying is going to cost £65,000 and you are borrowing £50,000. You want to buy the new place before you sell your present house. The new mortgage will not be available until you pay off the existing loan. So your 'bridge' would be £25,000 to get rid of the mortgage plus £15,000 for the difference between the new mortgage and the price of the house — a total of £40,000.

That sort of borrowing costs about £16 per day in interest — which is fine if it's only for ten days (£160); but imagine if the house doesn't sell after three months (£1,450) or worse, some defect unknown to you is putting off potential buyers, and you are stuck with it for a year. That is why banks are reluctant to make this 'layer' sort of bridging loan available.

3 What is 'gazumping'?

It happens when the seller of a house raises the price after agreeing it with you and accepting your offer. It is common during a period of intense house price inflation when a seller realises that, during the three months or so that it takes to deal with the sale, property prices generally will have risen — and his greed makes him rat on the agreement he made with you. It is a result of the system that there is no binding deal until exchange of contracts.

4 My offer for a house was accepted by the seller; the agent told me that I had to pay five per cent of the price as 'goodwill money' — a sort of deposit. Someone told me there is nothing legal about this and I don't have to pay it.

It's 'goodwill' money alright — for the estate agent, that is; he will put it on deposit and take the interest from it! And you are right — there is nothing 'legal' about it. Until contracts are exchanged, each side can back out and any deposit money paid is immediately returnable in full. So there is no need to pay it; it doesn't secure you as a buyer since the seller can always deal with someone else; and **he** is not sure of you because you can always change your mind. If you must pay something to keep everyone happy — just make it a nominal £100 or so.

5 Why does one pay a deposit anyway; isn't it just a formality?

Certainly not. When contracts are exchanged the buyer has to pay a lump sum of money — usually 10 per cent of the price (but it is negotiable) — to the seller's solicitor who will hold the money as 'stakeholder' until completion of the sale. There are three reasons for the deposit. First, it is an 'earnest of your good faith' — it

shows that you have a definite commitment which you
are prepared to back with real money. Secondly, if **you**
drop out after exchange you lose this money — which
is a very good reason not to drop out. It concentrates
your mind. Thirdly, if you back out, the seller will lose
money — legal fees, estate agents' commission, survey
fees on his purchase, deposit on his new house, and he
is entitled to keep the deposit you paid to pay his
losses. You can only get the deposit back if the deal
falls through because of some breach of contract by the
seller — discovering he doesn't own the house, for
example, or that he can't sell part of it. So don't treat it
as a mere formality — and do remember that you
actually need to have the money available

6   **Having made an offer on a house and had it
accepted, my building society valuation was
considerably less than the figure I had agreed
to pay; and their mortgage offer was
accordingly lower. Can I insist that the seller
reduces the price for the house?**

You can't *insist* on anything. The trouble with houses
is that they are worth what anyone is prepared to pay
for them. Your figure was what you thought was fair;
the building society valuer — who has a duty to
indicate what the likely price for the house would be if
the building society had to sell it in a hurry — thought
it was worth less than you did. The seller hopes to get
what you offered — or more. If you tell him you cannot
afford to go on unless he drops his price, he may stay
put and hope to get more on the basis that in many
parts of the country, prices are rising all the time. So —
you can go to the seller and tell him exactly what has
happened and ask if he will consider a reduction to
enable you to buy. He may agree. If you are convinced
that the price is right and that the property will
appreciate, you might try and raise the difference by a
bank loan or second mortgage. If you think of doing
this, do please make sure that the financial side is
within your ability to pay — particularly if something

goes wrong. Could you afford the loan if your wife/ husband was made redundant; or you started a family? Go into the money very carefully *before* you agree to exchange contracts and thus commit yourself irrevocably.

7 I am buying and selling but all my money is tied up in the house or will come from the new mortgage. I just don't have any spare cash to pay a deposit of more than a few hundred pounds. What can I do?

Well, you can ask your bank for a bridging loan (see Question 2 above); this should present no problem at all once you have got to the point of exchanging contracts on sale and purchase simultaneously. Or your solicitor can take out a short term insurance policy to meet the deposit. These schemes are quite new and it may take some time for them to catch on. You pay a flat rate single premium depending on the amount of the deposit required.

Your solicitor will also try to get the seller to agree a reduced deposit of, say five per cent (or less) instead of the conventional ten per cent. When that happens the seller usually says that if you default on the purchase, and fail to complete on the due day, the balance to make up ten per cent is immediately payable, a reasonable quid pro quo.

8 My solicitor says that I cannot use the deposit which my buyer is paying me to meet part of the deposit on the new house I am buying. Why on earth not?

There are two ways in which a deposit is paid to the solicitor for the seller. Either as 'stakeholder' — in which case he has to hold it 'frozen' until completion, and neither side can use it (the interest goes to the seller); or as 'agent for the vendor' — which means that the money immediately passes to the seller and he can do what he likes with it. Which method is used depends largely on what part of the country your solicitor works in. In London and the South East it is usual for 'stakeholders' to be insisted on; in other places 'agents' are normal. There is nothing to stop you trying to agree something different with the other side. When money is paid to the seller's solicitor as 'agent' there is always a risk that if the seller rats on the deal you will have difficulty in getting your money back; while if it had been paid to the solicitor as 'stakeholder' a cheque would be in the post. It is a small risk and one which most solicitors will advise their clients to take — provided the risk is explained.

9 What is the difference between freehold and leasehold?

Freehold means that you own the land for ever. A lease is 'carved out' of a freehold and is for a definite period — 99 years, 125 years (or even 999 years). It can be for a lesser period. Subject to one technical point (see following question) at the end of the leasehold period you have to hand back the whole caboodle and usually meet the cost of putting the place in good repair and decoration as well.

10 I own my house on a long lease; I thought I could buy the freehold.

Since 1967 there has been a right to buy the freehold or to extend the lease. This right applies only to **houses** — not flats. The lease must originally have been for at least 21 years and to qualify for the right to buy (or extend) you must have lived in the house as your residence for at least three years. It also covers properties which consist of a shop with living accommodation above — so long as the lease is for over 21 years and **you** live in the accommodation. Landlords are sometimes reluctant to sell, so there is a formal procedure of giving notice with a fall-back of applying to the county court for an order. You have to pay the landlord's legal costs and his surveyors fees — because there is sometimes argument about the valuation of the property. Whether it is worth doing depends on the length of the lease remaining, how long you intend to live in the house and what the landlord wants for the freehold. A 99 year lease retains its value for the first 40 years or so, then it slowly begins to become less valuable — with an acceleration in the last 15 years. It is also less easy to get a mortgage on a lease with less than 40 years to run — so it is worth getting good advice on the pros and cons of buying the freehold.

11 Do I need a solicitor to do the legal work when buying a house? Several of my friends did their own.

It is like any other specialisation; read it up and you can probably manage. It's fine so long as all goes well; it's the things you don't spot, or don't understand or which don't happen at all ('the dog which didn't bark in the night') which cause the headaches. And you will find that if you have a mortgage the lender will use his solicitor anyway — whose fees you will have to pay — and this may cause extra problems when he asks for information which you didn't think important. The lender's solicitor is only involved **after** exchange of contracts, when you only have about four weeks in which to get the whole thing done. If he raises some issue which you have overlooked but which you cannot answer, the money will not be available on completion day! However you may not actually save all that much on a purchase, but you will certainly save on the sale. You will only have to pay the lender's solicitors' fees for receiving the money and handing over the deeds. The real issue is whether **you** want the hassle of juggling your purchaser, his solicitor, your mortgagee and its solicitor, your seller, his solicitor and your new lender's solicitor — and trying to do your day job to earn the money to pay them all!

12 I am selling my house through an estate agent. Someone heard via a friend at work that the house was for sale and came to look at it. They made a very good offer and suggested that it was not worth involving the agents — thus saving their fees. Is this alright?

It all depends on the arrangement that you have with the agents and exactly how the 'buyer' learnt about the house. You may have given the agent 'sole selling rights' — which means that only he can sell the house; you can't even sell privately. In this case the deal you make with the 'buyer' does not cut out the agent; he is entitled to the fee anyway. Or you might have given him a 'sole agency'. This prevents you from employing another agent — the first can stop you by going to court if necessary. It is arguable that if you tell your pals that you are selling and ask them to 'spread the word' around — **they** are acting as agents for you. If you had a 'sole agency' agreement with the agent, he might just claim that there was some jiggery-pokery going on and demand his fee. And it is possible that the 'buyer' actually saw the agent's board outside the house and so

knew that it was for sale that way — in which case the
agent can claim his fee. If what happened is really pure
coincidence and the existence of the agent had no
bearing on the 'buyer's' decision **and** you have no
written agreement of the sort outlined — then you may
be in the clear.

13 While out house-hunting recently, we saw a house we liked and got the key from the agents. When we were leaving the house some more people arrived with a key and told us that they had already made an offer through a different estate agent. I thought you could only use one estate agent at a time?

No — you can be as prolific as you like. Opinions vary
about whether it is best to have a 'sole agency'
arrangement — in the forlorn hope that the agent will
devote his life to selling **your** house to the exclusion of
all the others on his books — or simply going to as
many agents as you can in the hope that by flooding the
market you will attract a firm buyer. There is some
evidence that by going to lots of agents the level of
service is lower — because the agents realise that there
is a good chance that someone else will get the fee.

14 Just when does the buying of a house become legally binding? Is it at the signing of contracts or when they are exchanged?

Signing the contract is merely putting your name on a
piece of paper. As contracts have to be 'exchanged',
each party has to **sign** some time in advance. So just
because you have **signed** does not mean very much.
    When each side is ready — you have your survey
report, mortgage offer, a firm buyer for your own place
and the money all arranged — your solicitor will tell
the seller's solicitor that you are 'ready to exchange'.
You have to agree a date for completion (which is
usually a Friday!) and then contracts are **exchanged**.
Sometimes it happens in person with each solicitor
actually handing over the contract. More often it is

done by a series of phone calls and the documents are
sent by post. Once contracts are **exchanged** the deal is
legally binding and enforceable.

15 What is the difference between 'registered' and
'unregistered' land?

In 1925 it was decided that all the land in the whole
country should be 'registered' with the State
guaranteeing the title to each separately owned bit of
land. Sixty and more years later we are still waiting —
although to be fair, a large amount of land **is** registered.
Practically all cities and large built-up areas and most
new housing estates are registered. But there are still
many properties in rural districts and smaller country
towns which are not. Registration only happens when
someone sells — so if a house has been in one family
for many years it may still be unregistered even though
it is in an area of compulsory registration. With a
'registered' title, all you have is a simple document

showing the owner and details of his mortgage (plus any restrictions or covenants affecting the land). The original is held at the Land Registry — so you can always get copies without difficulty. When land is 'unregistered' however, the owner (or his mortgagee) retains all the deeds going back for at least 15 years. It can be difficult sometimes to trace the originals of documents which are not handed on to a new buyer — as happens when you sell off part of a field, for example. You let the new owner have certified copies of the deeds showing your 'title' but retain the originals yourself.

One day all land will be registered and life will be a bit easier for everyone concerned with land transfer.

16 What happens if the deeds are lost?

It all depends on whether the title to the land is registered or not. If it is and you have lost the Land Certificate (as your proof of ownership is called) you can apply to the Land Registry for a duplicate. You have to pay a fee and there are various procedural hoops to be gone through (advertising for the missing certificate, for example) but eventually you will get a replacement without too much difficulty or expense.

If the title is unregistered you may have more problems. You have to be able to prove ownership for at least 15 years. Often you can 're-constitute' the title details from copies in solicitors' files. Failing that, you have to make a Statutory Declaration setting out when you bought the land and from whom and get supporting evidence from neighbours and perhaps your building society because they will have some record of when you took out your mortgage. And you will need to take out an insurance policy to guard against someone turning up in the future with the deeds and claiming to be the rightful owner.

17 Exactly what is 'title to land'?

It means legally acceptable proof of ownership of a piece of land. Property law is concerned **only with land** — though there may be a house or other buildings on it. The title depends on the unbroken chain of transfers from person to person being proved. Usually this is straightforward because there is a deed called a 'conveyance' which passes the whole of the land from A to B each time there is a sale. If an owner dies, there is a 'gap' in the chain which has to be properly filled by someone obtaining a grant of representation to show that he is lawfully able to deal with the land as executor, and to pass a good title on to the next owner.

18 Should a couple put the house in their joint names?

For most practical purposes — yes. There are two methods of joint-ownership which have different consequences. One is called 'joint-tenancy'. Here A and B own the property jointly and when one person dies, the survivor gets the **lot** simply by being the survivor. That is fine for most couples of modest means; each wants his or her spouse to be fully protected. The other method is called 'tenancy-in-common'; here A and B own the property jointly in the shares in which they bought it; but on the death of one his share does **not** go to the survivor — but passes on according to his will. This is used by wealthier couples as a way of trying to reduce the tax bill on death; or by unmarried couples who buy a house or flat jointly but have no desire that the other should make a windfall profit should one be run over by a bus. It is very important for the method of joint-ownership to be chosen wisely and for it to be explained fully to each person **before** signing on the dotted line.

19 I own my house jointly with my wife (we each have a quarter) and my mother in law, who has the other half. I want to sell the house to get our capital out and buy a smaller place but Mum won't agree. She says she is too old to be bothered. What can I do?

You can wait until she dies in which case you may become the owner (with your wife) of the whole house — assuming that the arrangement is a 'joint-tenancy'; or you can force a sale now. When two or more people own property jointly, the law regards this as a 'trust for sale' — that is, it is assumed that the intention of the buyers was one day to sell the place and divide the money up between them in the agreed shares. Of course that rarely happens in domestic dealing, but if there is a dispute which cannot be resolved, the court will always give effect to the 'trust for sale' and order that the house be sold. The dissenting owner has to obey and sign the necessary documents. Now going to court is probably the last thing you want to contemplate — but if Mum won't agree, that is your ultimate sanction. You could try and persuade her to see a solicitor who would explain to her what the law is and what could happen if she won't agree.

20 We live in a terraced house. The back of the house is separated from the garden by a path which gives access to other houses in the row. I know the path is a right of way — but can we put a gate across so long as the neighbours agree?

If all the people entitled to the right of way agree — fine. But blocking a right of way can cause problems. The question always is: Does the obstruction cause substantial interference with the right of other people to use the path? Putting up a gate which can easily be opened simply to keep your dog in — or stray children out — seems perfectly reasonable.

21 When I bought my house the solicitor muttered something about a covenant against business use, but I didn't really take it in. Now that I am redundant I want to operate a computer business from home but I'm worried about this 'covenant'. What is it all about? I thought my home was my castle?

A covenant is an obligation placed on a person — in this case the owner of a piece of land on which a house stands — to do or not to do something. You could have a covenant to put up and maintain a fence or allow someone to use your drains; those are 'positive covenants'. On the other hand there are 'restrictive covenants' which prevent you from doing something. Like building more than one house on a plot; or putting up a fence on an estate — or from carrying on any 'trade or business'. These may or may not be enforceable. It depends if there is someone around who has the 'benefit' of whatever it is you are not allowed to do. Not so long ago, a woman who owned a house on a modern estate which was subject to a ban on carrying on any trade started a baby-minding business — but the builder/developer was able to get a court order to stop her doing this. So whenever you buy property — do find out the extent and enforceability of any restrictive covenants which may run with the land you are thinking of buying. And don't think they are meaningless bits of legal jargon.

22 What happens if there is a 'restrictive covenant' stopping you doing something and you think it unreasonable?

You can always ask the other person if he will agree to the covenant being scrapped. If so — fine. If not, you can apply to the Lands Tribunal — a special court which deals with many aspects of land and compensation — and ask for the covenant to be modified or discharged. Whether this will be granted depends on the extent to which the person who has the benefit of the covenant is prejudiced and whether he can be adequately compensated in money for what he is giving up.

23 We are about to buy a house and it is being suggested that we have an 'endowment' mortgage rather than the ordinary repayment loan. What is the difference and are there any particular advantages in either method?

With a 'repayment' mortgage you borrow a lump sum of money and repay it with interest over, say, 25 years. At the end you get the deeds and a clear conscience. An 'endowment' mortgage is slightly different. You still borrow a lump sum of money but pay interest only on that loan for the 25 years. To enable you to repay the lump sum, you take out a life insurance policy to produce, on your death or at the end of the 25 years, sufficient money to cover the loan. When the 25 years are up you get the deeds and you may have some surplus from the life insurance proceeds. If you are intending to live in the same house for the whole 25 years it is probably not a bad idea. But many people move after a few years (the average life of a mortgage is only seven years). The value of the life insurance may be very small, if when you sell, you do not want to continue with it. You ought to do the arithmetic **very** carefully comparing the **total** cost to you of the two different systems and see if it is really worthwhile. Brokers and building societies may urge you to take the 'endowment' route — but ask them if that is because of the commission **they** earn rather than any real benefit to **you**.

24 When I bought my house I didn't have a mortage — and the solicitor insisted that I arranged insurance from exchange of contracts rather than completion some weeks later. Why?

Once contracts are exchanged there is a binding legal deal which you can enforce if the seller doesn't hand over the keys on completion day. Because of this, you have an 'insurable interest' in the property from exchange. If it burnt down and the seller was not insured (which is **not** unknown) you would be obliged to hand over your life's saving for a plot of land and a bit of smouldering rubble. So you must make sure that cover is on from exchange. With a mortgage, the lender will usually arrange automatic cover from that point.

25 I would like to take in a lodger to help with the bills when I buy my house. If I charge rent will this affect my mortgage?

Yes. Because of the complications which can arise under the Rent Acts, building societies are very chary about **anyone** else living in a house on which they are lending money. It is not impossible for the sort of arrangement you want to be worked out — but it is essential that you approach the building society **first** and tell them exactly what is proposed. Get their approval — **in writing** — before anything is done. It is for your own benefit too, because you don't want to find that you can't sell the house because your 'friend' has turned out to be a foe.

26 Our garden is bordered on the left by a fence which is in a dreadful state of repair — it looks dangerous to me. We have maintained the right-hand fence as we understood that was our responsibility. But the neighbour on the left refuses to do anything about it saying we can't prove it's up to him. How can we find out who is responsible?

Boundary fences are a nightmare. Very few house-owners indeed are actually **obliged** to maintain a fence. While in modern estates there are often covenants imposed on the owners making them responsible for upkeep — for older properties it is very rare. What usually happens is that it is **thought** that the fence on one side or the other belongs to the house. But just because it **belongs** does not mean that you have to maintain the fence. If your neighbour refuses to do the repairs, your only effective sanctions are either to persuade him to allow **you** to deal with **his** fence; or to erect your **own** fence a few inches on your side of the boundary. The deeds may give some indication of ownership but sadly usually not; if there **is** a duty to maintain a fence this will almost certainly be in the deeds. So it's worth retaining a copy of the deeds when you buy; or ask your building society to let you see them. They won't lend them to you in case you scoot off with them!

27 The house next door to us is rented out. It is in a very poor state of repair and there are rats about. Obviously we are worried that the rats will move to our property. We have talked to the landlord of the property till we are blue in the face, without any success. Surely he must keep the house in repair and deal with the rats.

There is no general duty to keep a house in repair; that's why you often see places falling apart at the seams, particularly in country districts. If you are badly affected by the lack of repair which causes dry rot or damp to come into your house from next door, you have a right to make a claim for damages for nuisance. The difficulty is that it is sometimes tricky to prove that the rot, damp, woodworm etc actually comes from next door. And as the landlord does not respond to a civil neighbourly approach, he may well be even less inclined to deal with your solicitors.

You can ask the Building Control Officer for the local authority to consider action under the Public Health Act if the building is dangerous or detrimental to the amenities of the neighbourhood because of its ruinous or dilapidated condition. He can serve a notice on the owner to do the work: And if he doesn't, the council can do it and send him the bill.

As for the rats, it's the responsibility of the owner of land to keep it free from rats. The council can serve notice on the bloke next door telling him to control the rats. Tell the Environmental Health Department that there are rats next door and ask for their help.

---

28 I want to put up a six foot high fence to make my garden more private. But my neighbour has a greenhouse which borders on the boundary. I don't think it will block out the light, but is there any law I should know about?

It depends how long the neighbour's greenhouse has been there. If it is more than 20 years, he may well have a 'prescriptive right' to light in a sufficient quantity to allow him to use the greenhouse for its ordinary purpose. If the period of use is less than 20 years, and he tries to prevent you building the fence — resist his objection on the ground that the law is definite about the 20 year minimum.

29 For the last ten years I have used a piece of land adjoining my garden to park the car. I want to build a garage on it and then within the next couple of years sell the house, garden and garage as one lot. Can I do this?

If you occupy a piece of land for twelve years without the owner's consent and without anyone claiming any rights over it, you acquire what is called 'title by adverse possession' (squatter's rights, to you). Once the twelve years have passed, you can safely do whatever you like and can sell the land as if you had acquired it by paying money for it in the more conventional way. So you must hang on for two years until you can show twelve uninterrupted years of use. Then build your garage and sell the land. Beware of asking the owner if he minds. Doing that shows that you still recognise him as the owner — and time stops running in your favour.

30 I have heard a rumour that there is to be a supermarket built near our home. Can we as residents object?

You can write to the planning department objecting — but you have to give 'planning' reasons for the objection: That there are sufficient shops of that kind; traffic difficulties — that sort of thing. Not just that you don't want it. You should also try and raise the thing as a community because that makes it easier for a common view to be expressed at any public enquiry. Also if a lot of people chip into a fund, it makes the legal costs less of a burden for individuals. The local press (and radio) may be interested in your objections.

31 There is a row of trees on my land on the boundary. The branches overhang next door's garden and their roots encroach on the next door garden. My neighbour says he wants to cut the trees back and he suspects that their roots may be growing under his garage causing cracks. Has he any rights?

Yes he has. He can cut off the branches which
overhang right back to the boundary (he has to give
back to you what he cuts off). He can cut the
encroaching roots off. If he can **prove** that it **is** your tree
roots that are damaging his garage, he can claim
damages from you too.

32 I want to alter the access to my garage by
making an opening onto the road. It means
cutting through the hedge but are there any
legal matters I should think about?

First check that your deeds don't prevent you from
opening the entrance through the hedgerow. Secondly,
and more importantly, you need to obtain planning
permission for any new access onto a public highway.
So get on to the Planning Department **before** you do
anything at all.

33 I live in a flat which is on a long lease (80 years
remaining) and there is a running battle about
service charges. Each year they are late in

preparing the accounts; there are disputes about the money spent on what we think are pretty poor services. When the outside was re-decorated we were not given any opportunity to get estimates from different contractors and were simply told to pay our share of the final bill. Is there any form of control on the managing agents and the landlords?

The law gives you some help by placing a limit on the right of landlords of blocks of flats to claim service charges from tenants. Items of work in the accounts can only be charged if they are of a reasonable standard and the expenditure on them must also be reasonable. If more than £25 multiplied by the number of flats or £500 whichever is the greater is incurred, two estimates must have been obtained and the expenditure must have been discussed with the tenants' association or if there isn't one, with individual tenants.

34 When I bought my house a lot was made of the need to do 'searches'. I never saw them and really don't know what it all meant.

There are three types of 'search' made when a house is bought. First, one searches at the Land Charges Registry to see if there are any 'charges' registered against the person selling. The person selling usually has the deeds among which will be a record of the first mortgage with which he bought the house. But any second or later mortgage which may have been taken out can only be protected by being registered at the Land Charges Registry. Also restrictive covenants, bankruptcy orders, and various types of court order may be registered against a person. And you really want to make quite sure that you know the true position early on so that any problems can be ironed out. Secondly, for land in the country you search at the Commons Registration Department of the County

Council to see if there is any common land or land subject to manorial rights among the property you are buying. Thirdly, you make searches and enquiries at the district council. This will reveal any matters affecting the plot of land you are buying, like planning restrictions, drainage, whether new roads are planned within 200 yards. It also says whether there are any 'local land charges'. These include things like improvement grants which still have to be repaid, bills incurred by the council under the Public Health Act, breaches of planning permissions. You need to know exactly what you are letting yourself in for, because this sort of charge runs with the land and is payable by the owner for the time being — even though it was some earlier person who incurred the liability. All these searches should have been shown to you by your solicitor before you exchanged contracts.

35 After I had bought my house I discovered that there was to be a nursing home in the very next building — a house which was newly converted and extended. No one bothered to find this out and tell me. What is the point of the searches if they don't reveal something as fundamentally important as this?

The searches and enquiries your solicitor makes relate to the **plot of land** you are buying. **Not** next door or at the end of the garden. It is important, therefore, that you make as extensive enquiries as possible by talking to the planning people, neighbours, chatting up the local traders. You can also ask the seller of your house point blank if he knows of any development, proposed by-pass, change of use or other possible change in the vicinity. If he says '**no**' but actually **did** know — you may later have a claim against him for damages, since you can say that his statement that nothing was planned induced you to enter the contract. The statement was wrong — it was a 'misrepresentation' which entitles you either to rescind the contract, which may be difficult if you have sold your old house, or to claim damages. But it is sometimes difficult and expensive to prove that he **knew**.

36 What are the costs and expenses of moving house?

On a sale — you have agents fees. These are usually a percentage of the actual selling price, anything from 1.5 per cent to 3 per cent depending on the price and the locality. VAT is on top of this fee. Or you may pay a lower fee but agree to meet advertising charges. The solicitor's fee on a sale is usually between 0.5 per cent and 1 per cent of the price, plus VAT. Removal expenses you can work out by getting estimates.

For the purchase, stamp duty at 1 per cent is charged on any house or flat costing more than £30,000. For registered land there is a sliding scale fee payable to the Land Registry which depends on the price. At £11,000 the fee is £20 and it rises by £5 for each £2,000 increase in price. Searches cost about £20. Solicitors charge about 0.5 per cent to 1 per cent of the price plus VAT — and usually include the cost of the mortgage. You can get a written estimate of costs from any solicitor before you start out and, of course you can shop around for quotes.

37 How do I find a solicitor?

Personal recommendation is by far the best way, because, if one of your friends has had a good experience, the chances are that you will be well served too. Ask your bank manager — he may know who to avoid! And building societies usually have their own 'pet' firms whom they recommend. Failing this, the Citizens Advice Bureau and libraries have a list of solicitors showing the type of work they do.

38 Once a sale has taken place, who pays off the mortgage and the agents fees etc; me or the solicitor?

The solicitor will have to discharge the mortgage because the deeds are only sent to him against his 'undertaking' — that means a binding promise — to pay off the mortgage out of the proceeds of sale. He has to obtain a receipt from the building society or bank who lent the money to hand to the buyer's solicitor proving that all debts have been cleared. It is usual for the agents' bill to be sent to the solicitor and for him to pay it. The balance of the proceeds of the sale should be sent to you on the day of completion — or a day or so later at the most. If you don't get the money, the solicitor should pay you interest on the money you have been denied.

39 I have a window and gutter which can only be reached from my next door neighbour's land. The deeds do not give me any right of entry and I don't get on with the chap next door. Is there any way I can demand entry?

If the deeds are silent — then the short answer is no. However unreasonable it may seem, the law entitles your neighbour to stand on his legal right and refuse you access. There has been a report by the Law Commission which recommends a new law giving a right of access to deal with preservation of your house, by cleaning gutters, painting etc on your promising to make good any damage you cause and indemnifying the neighbour against any loss or other liability. But this report has not yet been taken up by the Government. Until then — be nice to the people next door.

40 If this is right, how is it that tradesmen enter the garden and deliver mail, papers, milk etc?

Only because you have not stopped them. They have a 'licence' — a right to enter until such time as you withdraw it. That's why you see 'no hawkers; no tradesmen' signs on gates. They tell the world to keep out.

41 My solicitor told me that he was waiting for a 'bankruptcy' search to come in before he could complete my house purchase. What on earth has this to do with me?

It is actually very important. One of the things that is filed at the Land Charges Registry is notice that any person has been made bankrupt. This is vital, because a bankrupt person **cannot** buy or own land — therefore it is important for your building society to know **before** it hands over all the money whether or not you are bankrupt. When land is unregistered, one also checks

against the seller — for the same reason. If he **was**
bankrupt — he couldn't sell you the house.

42 When I was going round the house I hoped to
buy, the owner told me that he was moving
out. A few weeks later, before we had
exchanged contracts, he had indeed gone,
because I saw the removal van. But a day or so
later I was surprised to see a light on at night
and when I got the keys from the agents found
that a young couple were living there, I asked
them who they were and they said they had
been living in the house for about three years.
The agents were surprised. What should I do? I
can't get hold of the owner.

Immediately tell your solicitor and do not under any
circumstances exchange contracts. It is possible that
the couple are tenants and have rights of occupation. It
is the seller's problem to get rid of them because he has
to give you 'vacant possession'. Give him a week to let
you know precisely what the situation is. If there is no
sense from his side — think about buying another
house.

43 The Council have put up a lamp-post right in
front of my house, completely obstructing the
view from ground floor and bedroom
windows. It also shines away all night sending
a yellow glow all through the house. Can I get
it moved?

If you did, the chap down the road would then
complain and want it moved . . . and so on. There is a
statutory power for a local authority (which may be the
parish, district or county council) to erect lamp-posts to
light highways and streets. So long as the post does not
interfere with existing access to your property, the
council is acting properly. And you cannot try and
prevent the council unless you can prove that they are
not acting in good faith. You see, these powers have

been conferred by Parliament which is assumed to have taken into account the fact that adjoining land-owners (like yourself) might be adversely affected but have concluded that it is for the general good of the area that the lights should be put up. Of course if you can show that yours is the only house (or the last one) in the road and that by placing the lamp a few feet further away no one would be prejudiced but the street would still be well-lit — you may have a good case to put to the council. Otherwise — tough.

44 The road in which I live is a 'no-through road', at the end of which is a factory. That has a service road, but their vans and lorries are always racing up and down our road. We have written to the factory owners but to no avail. How can we try and get them to stick to their own service road?

Tell the local Highway Authority — which is probably your district council. Ask them to consider making a Traffic Regulation Order directing that only cars can use your road. That might be a nuisance for any of your neighbours who have their own vans of course. Tell the local police that there is a potential accident waiting to happen; the Superintendent may well be able to have a word with the factory people. Start up a campaign in the press and on local radio. Ask your local councillor for his help; that is one of the things you voted him into office for. Try and speak to the drivers of the offending vehicles and ask how they would feel if you drove up and down *their* road all day long. From a legal point of view there is not much you can do. As long as the road is a general purpose highway, anyone who wants has the right to pass and re-pass along it.

45 It seems that every time I hang my washing out on the line someone lights a bonfire in their garden. Is there any restriction on the time (or place) where you can have a bonfire?

Bonfires are an excellent idea — so long as it's your
own fire! There is no specific ban on lighting domestic
bonfires — they are not controlled by the Clean Air Act
or the Control of Pollution Act. But the normal law of
'nuisance' applies. If the person is *always* having a
bonfire or simply keeps one going all the time so that
neighbours are unable to use their gardens in a
'reasonable' way, you may have the makings of a legal
case against the person who is the pyromaniac. The
trouble is that the law also allows the neighbour to act
in a 'reasonable' way and he can have his fire so long
as he does not overdo it. The best way is to try and
negotiate with the chap. He may not realise that he is
causing you heartache and ruining your washing.

46

A neighbour keeps pigeons in his backyard.
They foul the roofs and gardens; apart from
being unpleasant, it is unsightly. He says there
is nowhere else he can put them. Is there
anything one can do about this?

In the country, farmers and landowners arrange shoots
to kill wild pigeons which cause a nuisance by eating
corn. And if tame pigeons stray on to farm land and eat
corn, the owner is liable to compensate the farmer for
the loss he sustains. This is not much help to you,
although if you can show that your garden or
paintwork suffers directly as a result of the constant
invasion of the birds, you may have a claim for
damages against the owner. The best bet would be to
ask the local authority to take action under the Public
Health Act. This enables the council to take any steps
to abate or mitigate nuisance, damage or annoyance
caused by 'congregation in built up areas of house
doves, pigeons, starlings or sparrows'. The birds can
be seized or destroyed (so long as it is done humanely).
There is also a product you can paint on ledges which
discourages birds from landing.

47 We live in a semi-detached house and share drainage facilities with the other half. The manhole cover for the drain is actually on their property. A blockage has occurred and we are in dispute about who is to blame. Whose responsibility is it to clean out the drain and to pay for the cost?

You probably cannot actually prove who caused the blockage. It could be virtually anything that was allowed to go round the bend and end up jamming the system; it might even be something that has happened to the drainpipe itself. Roots become entangled; cement fillets crumble; pipes actually crack or disintegrate. What is essential, of course, is that the thing is made to work properly as quickly as possible. That is in your interest as much as the people next door. So try and work something out amicably. Almost certainly the deeds will provide for a right for each owner to use the drainage system and to have access to each other's property to clean it out, repair it or maintain it. And the deeds usually say that each owner should meet half the cost. That is the fairest way. If it is necessary for any part of the drains to be repaired or replaced, it is essential that you and the chap next door *do* get on good terms and work out together the best firm to do the work. Perhaps he blames you for blocking the drain. If each of you can forget about who/what caused the blockage and look at the positive side of how to sort it out your mutual animosity should disappear.

48 I live in a basement flat on a 99 year lease. There is a larger flat upstairs and its owner is the only user of the steps up to what was the main front door. He did the conversion in fact. Water has been dripping through into my flat because the steps to the door are porous. The lease says that when there is to be any structural work or repair to the fabric of the house, I have to pay one-third; upstairs pays two-thirds. But the man upstairs refuses to do

**anything and says that he has no money. He
has a smart car, at least one wife and is
self-employed. What can I do to make him
meet his responsibilities?**

If he simply won't do anything, your only remedy is to
get the work done yourself, pay the bill and demand
two-thirds from 'him upstairs', suing him if need be. It
is obviously vital for you that the water damage is
stopped quickly, otherwise your flat will deteriorate.
Write him a letter saying what you are proposing to do
and asking him to agree now to meet his share of the
cost. Get a couple of estimates and let him see them.
Then, if he still does nothing — go ahead.

49 **I recently bought a house which was
advertised as having a 20 year guarantee for
some damp-proofing work. When we moved in
I found that there was some evidence of damp
on the flank wall — which was one of those
supposed to be treated. I wrote to the firm
which had done the work only to find that they
charged £40 to come out to look at what I was
complaining about. They also implied that the
guarantee was only available to the people
who had the work done originally. Is this sort
of thing allowed?**

The 'call-out' fee is certainly very common — although
it is not the sort of thing which is advertised in the
publicity about the firm nor in their guarantee
documents. The Office of Fair Trading has recently
been looking at these long-term guarantees and says
that while it may be reasonable to make some charge
for making a preliminary investigation (because the
problem *may* have nothing to do with the work that
was done and guaranteed) it thinks that some of the
fees are set deliberately high to discourage the use of
the very guarantee it is supposed to give. Whether the
document can be transferred from owner to owner
depends on what the guarantee says. In the majority of

cases, 'assignment' or transfer is allowed. There is a
case to be made for saying that non-transferable
guarantees are almost a deception, because it is known
that most people move house at least once in 20 years.

Everyday questions

1 My neighbour has a radio alarm which goes off every morning at 5 am. It is extremely loud and stays on for an hour. We have mentioned this to the neighbour several times, asking him to turn it down, but although he has been very polite he hasn't done anything. What course of action would you suggest?

Move. You may have legal remedies, but even if you make use of them and get a court order, you still have to live next door to the people and will be waiting on tenterhooks to see if they break the court's ruling. It is therefore much easier to find somewhere else to live than to put up with psychological warfare. Having said that, you can ask a solicitor to write to them pointing out that while it *may* be reasonable to have an alarm call at 5 am, it is *not* when it goes on for an hour; that is legally 'nuisance' and you would be entitled to ask a court to make an order stopping them acting in this way. The letter might achieve what you want — but it has been known for selfish neighbours deliberately to leave radios or noisy machines going all day simply to get back at the unfortunate complainer. That is why it is less nerve-wracking for most people with neighbour problems to move away.

2 We live next door to a pub. Every Saturday night without fail we are kept awake by slamming doors, music, yelling and tyres screaming away till about midnight. I realise that living by a pub is bound to be a bit lively — but surely what we suffer is unreasonable?

You can have a word with the police, because it may be that the pub is staying open beyond the permitted hours; and the owners of cars may be committing traffic offences. The best bet, however, is to get in touch with the Environmental Health Department because they have powers under the Control of Pollution Act to serve a 'noise abatement' notice on premises where there is excessive noise. The notice requires the people to stop ... or else they are taken before a magistrates court. Note that it applies only to *'premises'* — so you cannot use this Act to stop the din in the street. Finally, when the pub's licence comes up for renewal, you could object on the gound that the licencee is unable to control the people who leave last thing at night.

3   **The man next door is a DIY freak. He drills and hammers away every spare moment. And he revs up his car while tinkering with it on our shared drive. Is there any way of getting respite?**

Move. Although you could go to court for an 'injunction' (an order that he should stop what he does — or only do it 'reasonably'), you will have to share the drive and the party wall. There are some people who will not see reason. Their behaviour so irritates others that the problem becomes a personality issue rather than a legal one. Even if he stopped tomorrow, and gave up motoring, he would probably do something else which gets up your nose. Try reasoning with him. Keep taking him cups of tea. While he drinks it he will have to stop drilling; and the more tea he has the more frequent his 'comfort stops' will be — so you may get a breather that way!

4 At the end of our road is a football ground. Every Saturday there is a match and cars are parked all down our road, often on the pavement so that it is impossible to get by. We can never park anywhere near our house. Can we ask the police to put up 'no parking' signs?

Contrary to popular belief, there is no *right* for a house-holder to park his car in the road outside his house. You may do so if there are no parking restrictions, and if there is a space. But you can't block off part of the road. Even if there are no yellow lines or other restrictions, you can still be prosecuted for causing an unnecessary obstruction on the highway — if a fire engine could not get by, for example or a neighbour can't get his car out of the garage. Therefore anyone is at liberty to park along your road if there is room. They must not park on the pavement, and you could ask the police to deal with any drivers who do that. The police will only put up 'no parking' signs if *they* think that it is desirable. You might consider asking the local authority to make a 'Traffic Regulation Order' covering your road. This could ban parking altogether, or make it for residents only; there are a range of possibilities. But you might then find that *you* are in difficulty when Uncle Reg comes to tea and doesn't have a resident's parking permit — and so can't even park in the open space outside your gate.

5 My neighbour parks his car on the grass-verge in front of the houses. It's ruined the grass and made a real mess. He says he won't park on the road. Can we ask the Council (who own and maintain the verges) to do anything?

These grass verges were once regarded as a desirable public amenity and formed part of town planning layout. That was until everyone had cars. Your neighbour probably cannot park on the road — since he may be causing an 'unnecessary obstruction' by doing so and risk prosecution. What you can do is to ask the local council to make use of their power in the

Highways Act 1980 and to 'impose conditions on the
use of the verge' by directing the man to stop using the
verge to park his car. If he is served with this sort of
notice and refuses to comply with it he commits an
offence. If there is a general use of the grass verges for
car-parking (which is not uncommon) perhaps the
local residents should ask the council either to provide
more off-street parking; or to replace the grass with
concrete or, better still, create parking bays along the
road.

---

6   **Our neighbour parks a caravan in his front
drive. Quite frankly it's an eyesore in an
otherwise attractive area. How can we get him
to move it?**

You can't, unless it is a health hazard, which is
improbable. Your council may have bye-laws dealing
with the parking of caravans — but normally one is
allowed to park one caravan on one's own land. Does it
stop motorists from having a clear line of vision? If so,
the police might try and persuade the man to shift it
back a bit. Not much joy for you.

---

7   **At the end of our road is a derelict house. It
has been empty for years and the 'garden' is a
filthy mess of rubbish, weeds and all sorts of
unspeakable deposits. No one knows who
owns the place. Is there any way we can get
this eye-sore and health hazard seen to?**

You can ask the local council to take action under the
Public Health Act. They should know who owns the
place, since someone will be sent a rate demand every
year. The council can tell the owner to tidy it up — or
they can do it themselves and reclaim the cost from
him.

---

8   **Is there any way of finding out just who does
own a house or land? I would quite like to buy
a piece of ground adjoining my garden but I
have no idea who owns it.**

There is no formal way, if that's what you mean. The
Land Registry is not open to the general public; they
will give out details only if you have the owner's
consent. There is a proposal to change this and do
away with the secrecy. That would only cover
registered land, of course. The best bet is to ask around
the locality. Find someone who has lived there for
many years; old inhabitants often know a great deal
about the place they live in. Or you could put an advert
in the local paper. A long shot, that one, since if the
owner is not local, he may never see the paper. But
someone who *does* know may reply.

9 We live near a fish and chip shop. We are fed
up with the litter left lying around the street —
old newspapers, greasy chip wrappers etc. The
fish-shop owner says he provides a litter bin
outside the shop but isn't responsible apart
from that. Can we do anything?

There was a story of a motorist throwing an empty
cigarette packet out of his car window on to the
pavement in Cheltenham. An elderly lady picked it up
and handed it to him. "Thank you", he said, "but I
have no further use for it"; "Neither has Cheltenham"
replied the lady. It is an offence to leave litter at any
place in the open air to which the public have free
access; so you can take action against any person
whom you see dropping litter — if you know their
name and address. You can ask the owner to empty the
bin more often and also ask the council to consider
placing extra litter bins in the vicinity. We are just a
filthy nation, that's the real trouble. Children are not
taught to take their sweet papers, comics, etc home
with them.

10 I read about a man being taken to court for
attacking an intruder. Surely if someone
breaks into my house I can tackle him in any
way I want?

Not so. It may seem daft — but you can only take such

action as is 'reasonable' when confronting an intruder.
So if he is not violent *you* cannot act violently —
simply ask him to leave, taking his arm to encourage
him perhaps. If he is armed with any sort of weapon,
you can retaliate to the same degree as the force with
which he is threatening you. But if you do shoot at
someone, or hit him too hard, *you* may end up in the
dock.

11 My father bought me an 'anti-rape' device — a spray/alarm — to carry but a friend says that they are illegal in this country. Surely this can't be right?

If you have any article in a public place which is made
or adapted to be used for causing injury — you commit
an offence. These sprays are intended to injure an
attacker, so they are illegal. However in a very recent
case, a girl, although convicted of the offence, was
given an absolute discharge by the magistrates.

12 Does this extend to defending yourself generally? I read of a woman who was attacked and used her nail scissors against her attacker, only to be prosecuted.

Anything, however innocent, can turn into an
'offensive weapon'. And a weapon carried for self-
defence if you are attacked *is* an 'offensive' weapon as
it is intended to be used to cause injury. The Courts
have held that frightening or intimidating an attacker is
'causing injury'. The logic of prosecuting the
unfortunate victim of a deliberate attack seems odd.

13 A friend bought an air-gun as there have been a lot of burglaries in the area and says that if he finds anyone breaking in, he'd use the gun. Would he be committing an offence?

Yes, certainly — unless the attacker was also carrying a
gun and threatened to use it against your chum.

14 What is the difference between a Solicitor, a Lawyer and a Barrister?

'Lawyer' is the generic name for solicitors and barristers. There is no separate creature!

A Barrister is a lawyer who works on his own and appears in the courts as an advocate, defending or prosecuting people accused of crimes; representing one side or the other in civil proceedings — like personal injury claims, divorces, disputes over wills. And Barristers also specialise in different branches of the law and advise people expertly. They can only be contacted via Solicitors.

Solicitors are lawyers who usually work in partnership with others and are the general practitioners of the legal world. They have daily contact with clients on a wide range of legal problems and can also appear in the lower courts as advocates. While they get involved with legal disputes and defend people on criminal charges, much of their work is not contentious — like house purchase and sale, wills, probate, tax advice and planning, company formation and welfare and benefit advice. Every high street has one; so should every citizen!

15 I have been called for Jury Service — am I obliged to go and what happens to the wages I lose when I am not at work?

Yes — you *MUST* attend court — otherwise you can be fined. There are some people who are exempt from jury service — all judges, solicitors, barristers and their staff; ministers of religion; the mentally ill. Peers, medical people and members of the forces can ask to be let off — and people who have been to gaol for longer than five years are disqualified. If you are by chance within these categories, you should tell the court which summoned you. You are paid subsistence and travelling expenses and loss of pay on a daily basis.

If the task of serving on a jury causes you hardship —

because you are self-employed, for example, or you
have arranged to go away for a holiday — you can ask
to be excused. And if you are related or known to
anyone in the dock you *must* notify the court.

16 A 'friend' has owed me money for over a year
now and despite his promises, no money is
forthcoming. What is the small claims court
and is it relevant to my position?

It depends. Actually, there is no such thing as a 'small
claims' court. There is the High Court — where one
sues for large debts over £5,000. And there is the
county court for claims up to £5,000, (although you can
sue for larger amounts if the other side agree). Within
the county court there is a special procedure for claims
up to £500. These will be dealt with by the court
without lawyers and the winner will not be allowed
any legal fees if he uses a solicitor. This 'do-it-yourself'

scheme has become known as the 'small claims procedure'. It is supposed to be easy for an individual to make a claim on his own without legal advice and guidance. So what you do depends on how much your ex-friend owes you. If it is over £500 it may be sensible to go to a solicitor and get him to start proceedings to claim the money. If it is less, you will have to do it yourself. There is a booklet available from the county court which explains what you have to do. Remember that you have to be fairly certain before you start that the debtor has the means to pay; otherwise it's a case of blood out of a stone.

17 I recently sued someone who owed me money. The court fee was £35. As soon as he got the summons he offered to pay me the debt and I agreed to withdraw the action. But the court refuses to repay the fee. How do I get my money back?

You don't. The system has trapped you. What you should have done when the man offered to pay was to say that you would accept instalments (or whatever he proposed) on condition that he paid the court fee and agreed to the action being 'adjourned generally'. Then, if he had not paid, you could bring the action to life again. So apart from asking the man to meet the court fee as a matter of honour, there is not much you can do. You could apply to the court to say there has been a compromise without any reference to costs; but if your withdrawal of the action was done in a formal way by filing a notice of 'discontinuance' — you have had it.

18 I agreed to be a guarantor for a pal at work. I lost touch with him when he moved away but his bank has been on to me saying that he has done a bunk and that I should pay what is owing. Surely they should chase *him* — not me.

What has happened is precisely the reason for the bank wanting a guarantor. If the principal debtor (your pal) makes off, the creditor (the bank) is entitled to pursue you (the guarantor) for everything that is outstanding. You have a claim against the man, but finding him and making a legal claim is *your* problem — not the bank's. Ask the bank to tell you where the man can be found so that you can get in touch with him; but you must come to some arrangement with the bank as soon as possible. Otherwise interest and costs will mount up.

Moral: Never agree to be a guarantor for anyone unless you know them very well.

19 How can I get legal aid to bring a case against someone who damaged my car?

First — how much are you claiming? If it is less than £500 you won't get legal aid at all. If it is a larger amount you should see a solicitor and ask him to advise you whether you come within the scope of legal aid. There is a means test and qualification depends on how many dependents you have, what your outgoings are and, of course, what you earn. It is *always* worth seeing if you qualify. If there is little chance of actually getting the money you are claiming, you may find the Legal Aid committee reluctant to allow you to bring the action, since it would be a waste of public money. If you have savings these may be taken as a contribution towards the legal aid — and you often have to pay by instalments part of your earnings towards the bill.

20 I think my solicitor has overcharged me for the conveyancing work he did when I bought my house; and he deducted what was 'due' from the money he received from the mortgage people. Can I complain and if so to whom?

First — have you raised it with your solicitor? He may agree that the bill is higher than you might have been led to believe and make a reduction himself. Next, you can write to your solicitor and ask him to obtain a 'remuneration certificate' from The Law Society (the solicitors' ruling body). The Law Society will call for the solicitor's file, bill and for full details of what he did. You will have an opportunity to put your point of view. They then issue a certificate saying what they would regard as a fair charge. While it is normal for a solicitor to deduct his charges from money in hand, equally he should first have agreed those charges with you and obtained your agreement to the deduction.

21 How does one become a magistrate?

You can apply to the Local Advisory committee which is set up by the Lord Chancellor. Your local magistrates' clerk will put you in touch. There is a form you complete and the matter is then considered in private by the committee. You may or may not receive an invitation to become a magistrate. A lot of people object to the 'secrecy' but that is the way the system works at present. The committee tries to have a number of magistrates whose political views reflect the general opinion in the area; they need to have women as well as men. Candidates must be prepared to devote time both to being available on the bench and to attend training courses to keep up to date with the law.

22 I was sent to prison a long time ago. Is it right that I can now refuse to say that I have a record and can ignore questions about it on forms?

The Rehabilitation of Offenders Act 1974 says that once a person has been 'rehabilitated', *no* use can be made of his conviction in civil courts, tribunals, arbitration or disciplinary proceedings; and there is *no* need to refer to it in job applications or when applying for insurance. BUT — it *can* still be referred to in criminal cases, in applications for certain types of job — for example, doctor, lawyer, dentist, police, prison service, work with children under 18 and some types of insurance (eg fidelity bonds). And it *can* be mentioned in adoption, child care and divorce cases.

When are you rehabilitated?

Prison	6 months to 2½ years	after 10 years	half if
Prison	up to 6 months	after 7 years	you were
Fine		after 5 years	under 17
Borstal		after 7 years	
Detention centre		after 3 years	
Remand home/approved school		1 year after end of order	

There is *NO* rehabilitation for sentences of more than
2½ years, life sentences or detention during Her
Majesty's pleasure.

23 Can a policeman stop you when you are driving and make you take part in a traffic census?

Yes he can, if the census or survey is being done on or
near the road on which you are travelling. However,
you cannot be forced to participate in the survey and if
you tell the policeman that you are 'unwilling to
furnish any information for the purposes of the survey'
— he must not cause you unreasonable delay.

24 In our part of the country there are a number of United States bases and troops. Recently cars were stopped by American soldiers in uniform and there were no police about. Is this legal?

Not unless there were police very close by and the troops were acting in conjunction with them. There is no power for soldiers (of any nationality) to stop the general public using the highway, unless they are working with the civil police. Write to the Chief Constable of the force in question asking him if he knows that this has taken place on his 'patch'. You could also bring a claim for false imprisonment against the soldiers — if they actually prevented you going on when you wanted to.

25 What are all these 'Ombudsmen' one hears about?

There are three different types. The first, in this country, is the 'Parliamentary Commissioner'. He has the power to investigate complaints of maladministration by government departments directed to him only by Members of Parliament. You *can't* approach him direct. If a complaint is found to be justified, he can direct the department concerned to compensate you.

The second category consists of the two Commissions for Local Administration for England and Wales. They can investigate complaints against local councils by any individual or group. The trouble is that although the commissioners may find that the local authority *was* guilty of maladministration — they have no power to *make* them give you redress.

The third group are 'private' ombudsmen whose powers have been created outside Parliament. There is one for insurance; one for banking and there will shortly be one for building societies. The Insurance Ombudsman is only able to deal with complaints about companies who subscribe to the scheme; not all do. One important point about both the insurance and banking schemes is that *before* you approach the ombudsman, you *must* have referred your problem to a senior person in the insurance company or bank concerned.

26 Can you explain the difference between 'bankruptcy' and 'liquidation'?

'Bankruptcy' is for people. When a person is unable to pay his debts a creditor can make him 'bankrupt'. This means that all his property and assets are taken over by a trustee who tries to sort out the debts and devise a scheme for repaying them out of capital and from the bankrupt's wages or other income. When a *limited company* is unable to pay its debts (or is 'insolvent') it goes into 'liquidation'. The main difference is that for a bankrupt person, his obligation to repay lasts (in theory) for ever. But when a company goes into liquidation, the liquidator realises the assets and pays off what he can. Then that is it. There is no continuing liability because once a company is bust it ceases to exist for all practical purposes — whereas a person goes on living and can earn money to pay off his debts as time goes by.

27 I have been at my new job for two months now but still haven't received a contract. Can I insist on getting something in writing?

Yes. When you are not given a written contract before your job starts, you are entitled to be given a statutory 'written statement of the terms and conditions of your employment' within 13 weeks of your starting work. (This does not apply if you are a part-time worker, working less than 16 hours a week.) The terms have to set out your hours, pay, job description, holiday entitlement, pension and notice provisions as well as disciplinary rules and procedures. You can complain to an Industrial Tribunal if your employer won't comply with this simple rule.

28

I applied for promotion after working my way up the company. Totally unexpectedly, the position was given to someone who is far less experienced than I and was only recently employed by the company. I am convinced that this was because I am a woman (the succesful applicant is a man). There are no further promotion prospects and I feel my future is uncertain. Is there anything I can do?

You think you are a victim of sex discrimination. You probably are. The problem is proving it. You can take your case to an industrial tribunal, but before you do, you should get in touch with the Equal Opportunities Commission. They have the power, in certain cases, to support a person who is a victim of discrimination. Certainly they will explain to you what you have to be able to do to try and convince a tribunal that there was deliberate unfairness in the way the job vacancy was filled.

29

After 15 years in one job I left quite amicably and had a break. Now, when I apply for a new job and give my old firm as a reference, it appears that they are telling people that I was a bad time-keeper and poor worker and that was why I left. Surely references should be honest?

Certainly they should — but they can also be frank. What you have to do is get hold of a copy of the letter which you say contains untrue statements and see a solicitor about it. You will need to be able to bring some evidence from fellow-workers at your old place that you were *not* a bad time-keeper; if you had a clocking system there should be very accurate records which the company might have to produce should the case ever go to court. You may have a claim for libel if the reference is completely inaccurate.

30

What do I do if I think I was sacked unfairly?

First, you must have been employed for at least two years before you have any right to bring a claim under the Employment Protection (Consolidation) Act. Secondly, you must bring your case to an industrial tribunal within three months of the date of your dismissal. Reasons for dismissal include redundancy, and your conduct, capability or qualifications, the onus being on the employer to show that the dismissal *was* fair. When you apply to the tribunal, they will give you guidance; and also a conciliation officer will see if a compromise can be agreed — or, if you have no hope at all, tell you so. It is worth seeing a solicitor quickly if you are sacked because there may be legal remedies for breach of contract which are worth pursuing even if you can't go to tribunal.

31

My wife has been taken into hospital with a mental illness. The house is in our joint names but I want to sell it and move to be nearer to her. How can I deal with the sale?

If your wife is suffering from an illness which makes
her incapable of managing her own affairs or of
understanding what is going on, you will have to apply
to the Court of Protection yourself (or by some other
close relative) as 'receiver' for your wife. This takes a
little time and also costs you money each year, but until
she recovers that is the only way forward. Before you
go to the Court, do ask the Medical Superintendent at
the hospital to tell you whether your wife is capable of
understanding a contract for the sale of her house and
if there is any chance of quick recovery. If he says 'yes'
it may be worth waiting until she is better.

32 We went out for a walk in the country following footpaths marked on the Ordnance Survey map. One particular footpath which was marked on the map as a public right of way was fenced off with a 'No Trespassing' notice. Is this legal?

If the footpath *is* still open to the public — that is, no
closure or diversion has taken place — it is quite wrong
for anyone to try and stop you using it. Indeed, it is a
criminal offence to put up a sign to deter you from
lawfully using the path. You can check with the
Highways Department of your County Council whether
the footpath is still in use and is on the definitive map
of the district.

33 Can I record films and records on tape? What happens about the copyright?

If you want to tape music from a record you will be
breaking the copyright of the company who made the
record in the first place. You can get round this by
buying a licence from the Mechanical Copyright
Protection Society. At present there is no scheme for
permitting general recording of films and television on
video. You have to ask the owner of the copyright of
the film or approach the BBC or ITV company.

34 What about playing radios or tapes in a shop?

If you play music from a radio or television the
composer or publisher of the music is entitled to a
royalty payment because you are making a public
performance of his work. The Performing Rights
Society looks after the interests of those concerned and
collects royalties by levying licences on any trader who
wants to use a radio or TV in his shop or garage or any
other trade premises. The money is then distributed
among all composers and publishers. The fee payable
depends on the size of the premises and the amount of
music.

   If music comes from records or tapes (but *not* from
radio or TV) a licence is required by the recording
company whose record or tape is being played.
Phonographic Performance Ltd have a range of licence
fees which should be bought before the music is
played.

35 I have a computer and I saw in the paper that I should have a licence for something; can you explain?

The Data Protection Act 1984 is one of the least
intelligible bits of law in recent years. Typical of
anything to do with computers, one might think! The
intention behind the Act is that the public should have
access to computer records about themselves (which is
fair enough). So that the public know who may hold
this information, computer users must register with the
Data Protection Registrar. Exempt from registration is
personal data held by an individual and concerned
only with the management of his personal, family or
household affairs, or held for recreational purposes
only. Also probably exempt is data held by clubs
relating only to club membership, and lists of names
and addresses held on a computer. There are limited
exemptions for data held by employers for pay-roll
purposes. The trouble is that many people hold more

general data about individuals — voting preferences, where they went to school, age, employment, hobbies — all of which will take the computer owner outside the exemption. The best advice is to write and tell the Registrar what information you hold, and for what purposes, and ask if he thinks you should register. Computer bureaus also have to register.

36 Why it is that some shops can open on a Sunday and others cannot?

Because there is a law which says so. The Shops Act 1950 lays down very clearly just who can and cannot open. The Act is enforced by local councils — some of whom are very tough, though others appear to turn a blind eye. There is a wide range of places that *can* open — largely concerned with the sale of food and drink, newspapers, car parts and petrol (NOT cars), railway bookstalls, guidebooks and souvenirs at museums etc, sports equipment (at a place where the sport is played) and fodder for horses. Bread, fish and groceries may be sold (up to 10 am) in a shop where the local council has made an exemption order. And a local authority may designate an area as a 'holiday resort' and permit shops to be open for not more than 18 Sundays in a year to sell bathing and fishing articles, photographic requisites, toys, souvenirs and fancy goods, books etc and any article of food. Apart from these permitted exemptions, NO SHOP MAY BE OPEN ON SUNDAY for the serving of customers. So garden centres, DIY shops, furniture stores, car salesrooms and many other places to which people gaily go on a Sunday are open illegally. Over 20 attempts have been made to reform the law, the latest following a very comprehensive report which said that all restrictions should be scrapped. But the Bill to change the law was thrown out.

37 A man came and took a picture of my house. I have no idea what he will do with it; he might have been a burglar 'casing the joint'. Have I any right to get hold of the negative?

No. There is no law of privacy, nor can you stop people taking a picture of your house — nor of you, or your dog for that matter. If he looked like a burglar 'off-duty', you could tell the police, assuming you kept a note of his description and car; (did you take *his* photo?). Nothing else you can do.

38 Can anything be done to stop estate agents putting up boards all over the place, defacing the street? Some houses in my area are in the hands of more than one agency and so there are several boards with different names all advertising the same place. This seems to be a recent development. Can I complain about it?

Estate agents' boards advertising flats to let and houses for sale are 'advertisements' and may be controlled by the Town and Country Planning (Control of Advertisements) Regulations 1984. These rules say that consent should be obtained from the local council. There is an exemption for temporary adverts relating to the sale or letting of land. But if there is a forest of such adverts, the council may take action against the estate agents concerned. There is a limitation on the size of the board (one must not be larger than 2 sq metres — two not more than 2.3 sq metres) and the sign must not project more than one metre. So tell the local planning department and ask them to take action.

39

Is there any way in which I can find out just who is my landlord? I pay rent to an estate agent who says he is 'uncertain' and seems to me to be deliberately evasive.

Some landlords wish to remain 'incognito' for reasons of ther own — it's difficult to make them repair property or deal with problems if you don't know who they are. And they may wish to trouble the Inland Revenue as little as possible. The law now says that a tenant is entitled to ask for a written statement of the name and address of the landlord by writing to the person who demands or receives the rent. Failure by this agent to give the details within 21 days is a criminal offence. If the landlord is a limited company, the receiver of the rent must give the name of the company, the name and address of its secretary and of every director. The local authority can prosecute the agent if he fails to answer your questions.

40

Are we governed by European Law or only by the law passed by the British Parliament?

The main part of European law is the Treaty of Rome — which sets out the main objectives of the European community and the way in which they are to be achieved. It also set up the European Court of Justice. New laws come from the EEC as 'Directives' and these *have* to be incorporated into our law by Parliament — either as Acts or, more commonly, by Regulations. When there is a point of law which is unclear, the

British courts can refer it to the European Court whose decision is binding not only on us but on all other Member States.

41 I keep being phoned up by people trying to sell me things. Is there any way in which I can prevent my name and address being used in this irritating way?

Only by going ex-directory — which may be as big a nuisance. Telephone selling is big business and so long as phone numbers are generally available — it's an easy way to try and make contact. Usually the people are trained to respond sensibly and politely if you say you are not interested. If you are getting 'junk mail' you can try and get your name and address off the mailing list by applying to 'Mailing Preference Scheme' Freepost 22, London W1E 7EZ. But this won't take you off all the lists. Keep all the unwanted mail for scrap — and use it for church/village/school funds.

42 How long can you be held at a police station without being charged?

It depends why you are at the police station. If the police are investigating an 'ordinary' crime, there is a general principle that you cannot be kept in police detention without charge for more than 24 hours. However, the same law that gives that right of protection of the liberty of the subject goes on to enable a senior police officer (a superintendent or above) to authorise your continued detention for a period of up to twelve hours. To justify such an authorisation, the police officer must have reasonable grounds for believing that three conditions are met: (a) that the extra detention is necessary to get evidence through questioning; (b) that the offence is a *serious* one; (c) that the investigation is being done diligently and expeditiously. Alternatively, the police may go to a magistrates court and ask them to authorise further detention for up to 36 hours and to extend it to a further

36 hours — making 96 hours in all. So, in summary, the police may detain you for 36 hours on their own; magistrates may extend this to a maximum of 96 hours.

If you are in custody on a terrorism investigation, the police may detain you for 48 hours initially and the Home Secretary can extend this by order by such periods as he may think appropriate up to five days. The maximum detention period is therefore seven days.

43 Have you any right to see a lawyer during police detention?

Now you do. There is a statutory right to request to be able to communicate and consult privately with a solicitor while you are in police detention. You must be held in custody — and *you* must request the presence of a solicitor. If you have not got your own, one will be found who will see and help you on legal aid. Once you have requested a lawyer, the interrogation cannot continue (unless the police have grounds for believing that the delay would be prejudicial to the investigation of the offence).

A senior police officer may delay the consultation if you are detained for a serious offence; this delay may be for a maximum of 36 hours. It is your right to see the lawyer in private and to have him present at the police interview.

This right extends to people in detention for terrorism offences except that then the consultation may only take place in the sight and hearing of a police officer in uniform.

44 I hired a van for a day and agreed to return it to the hire firm when they opened at 8.00 the following morning. I was stuck in heavy traffic and I could not get to the depot until 8.30. They said I had to pay a further day's hire charge. Surely they cannot do this?

Why not? Your contract was for a 'day' and this equals 24 hours. In addition you specifically agreed the return time. Winston Churchill would have said that you should have started earlier to allow for traffic delays, breakdowns etc. Or you should have made enquiry about any leeway for returning the van a bit late. Many firms allow you up to an hour or so without penalty, or make a charge of a proportion of the day's hire rate. It is worth shopping around when you are thinking of hiring and reading the 'small print' which is thrust in front of you to sign when you are collecting the vehicle.

45 I have a motor insurance policy which runs from February each year. The annual premium is payable by twelve 'direct debits' from my bank account. I received the certificate of insurance on time but after three months no money had been debited from my account. I am worried that the insurance might be invalid. What can I do? I have phoned the insurance company several times but nothing has happened.

First — don't worry. The motor insurance *is* in force and is perfectly valid for all purposes. Secondly, *write* to the manager of the local branch of the insurance company telling him what is happening (or rather *not* happening). This should result in the money being collected properly. If still there is no joy, take the matter up with the Chief General Manager of the company. It may be that there is a fault in their systems which means that there are lots of people in your position, and he will be glad to know and to put it right. If you will find difficulty in having three (or more) months payments lopped off your account, tell the insurance manager to re-arrange the payments so they are spread more evenly over what is left of the year. It's possible that you have one of those good old fashioned policies where after many years of faithful payment you get a 'free' year. But probably not!

46 I have invented a toy for children. It took me several months of thought and trial and error before I came up with a prototype. Although I

**would love to develop and sell the toy myself I
simply cannot afford it and would not know
how to go about it anyway. What is the best
thing to do? Should I patent it and sell the
rights?**

Patenting something is far from easy. It is costly even if
you do it yourself because there are fees payable to the
Patent Office initially for 'searches' (to see if there is
anything similar or even identical already on the
register); and if your invention *is* patented, annual fees
are payable for the 20 year protection period which the
patent gives you. There are several grounds which stop
you from getting a patent anyway — that the invention
is not new or that it was obvious; games and computer
programs are excluded. So for you to exploit your new
toy the best thing is to try and get a company which
makes children's toys to take up your idea. The best
thing would be to find the leading companies and write
to them asking first if they would be interested *and*
prepared to sign a document promising not to breach
your confidence. You may find that some firms will not
agree. Avoid them. If you get a positive response, get
your 'breach of confidence' document signed — *then*
show them your design. If they are interested, they may
offer you a fee for the idea plus a royalty on sales. Make
sure you get good legal advice on any contract which is
sent to you to sign BEFORE you commit yourself.

47 **I placed an advertisement in the local paper. It
was very important that the ad. appeared on
the day I requested, since I took time off work
to be at home and cope with what I hoped
would be a flood of interested callers. Nothing
happened and I looked at the paper to find to
my horror that the advert was not in that day.
When I phoned they said it was a mistake and
they would re-print it free. But I have lost a
day's pay needlessly. What can I do?**

Write to the Managing Editor of the paper and tell him

exactly what happened and how much you have lost.
Explain to him that you specifically wanted that day's
paper because you were taking time off and that this
was made quite clear to the person who took the advert
in. Then go on to say that the newspaper is in breach of
its contract with you and that you are claiming the
day's pay as 'damages'. See what happens. It is very
likely that you will receive a lame excuse coupled with
a denial of liability for this sort of 'consequential loss'.
You may be referred to the paper's terms and
conditions of acceptance of advertising copy — which
you may well not have seen nor had drawn to your
attention *before* placing the advert. If this is the case,
the terms and conditions do not apply to your contract
and any exclusion of liability is of no effect. Assuming
that the money is not sent to you, the only remedy is for
you to sue them in the local county court for your loss
of pay. Whether you wish to face the worry of that is
another matter — one which they no doubt take
advantage of when rejecting your proper legal claim.

Advertising Standards Authority
Brook House
2-16 Torrington Place
London WC1E 7HN
01-580 5555

Association of British Travel Agents
55-57 Newman Street
London W1P 4AH
01-637 2444

British Insurance Association
Aldermary House
10-15 Queen Street
London EC4N 1TU
01-248 4477

British Standards Institution
2 Park Street
London W1A 2BS
01-629 9000

Citizen's Advice Bureau
700 branches around the country;
see local Yellow Pages

Commission for Racial Equality
Elliot House
10-12 Allington Street
London SW1B 5EH
01-828 7022

Companies Registration Office
Companies House
Crown Way
Maindy
Cardiff CF4 3U2
0222-388588

Consumers Association
14 Buckingham Street
London WC2N 6DS
01-839 1222

County Court
see local Yellow Pages

Equal Opportunities Commission
Overseas House
Quay Street
Manchester M3 3HN
061-833 9244

Health and Safety Commission
Regina House
259-269 Old Marylebone Road
London NW1 5RR
01-723 1262

Independent Broadcasting Authority
70 Brompton Road
London SW3 1EY
01-584 7011

Insurance Ombudsman Bureau
31 Southampton Row
London WC1B 5HJ
01-242 8613

Land Registry
32 Lincoln's Inn Fields
London WC2A 3PH
01-405 3488

Law Society
113 Chancery Lane
London WC2
01-242 1222

Legal Aid
P.O. Box 9
Nottingham NG1 6DS

Mailing Preference Scheme
1 New Burlington Street
London W1E 7EZ
01-378 7244

Mechanical Copyright Protection Society
Elgar House
41 Streatham High Road
London SW16 1ER
01-769 4400

Motor Insurer's Bureau
Aldermary House
Queen Street
London EC4N 1TR
01-248 4477

National Consumer Council
18 Queen Anne's Gate
London SW1H 9AA
01-222 9501

National Council for Civil Liberties
21 Tabard Street
London SE1 4LA
01-403 3888

Office of Fair Trading
Field House
15-25 Breams Buildings
London EC4A 1PR
01-242 2858

Patents Office
State House
66-71 High Holborn
London WC1R 4TP
01-831 2525

Performing Right Society
29-33 Berners Street
London W1
01-580 5544

Phonographic Performance Limited
Ganton House
14-22 Ganton Street
London W1
01-437 0311

Royal Institution of Chartered Surveyors
12 Great George Street
Parliament Square,
Westminster
London SW1P 3AD
01-222 7000